D1597586

What Is Said to the Poet Concerning Flowers

What Is Said to the Poet Concerning Flowers

BRIAN KIM STEFANS

FACTORY SCHOOL
2006

PREVIOUS APPEARANCES OF SOME OF THESE POEMS:

Arras: "Verl," *Asian Journal:* "The Window Ordered to Be Made," *Best American Poetry 2004:* "They're Putting a New Door In," *Boston Review:* "They're Putting a New Door In," *Brooklyn Rail:* "Idea for Poem," *Callaloo:* "Les Assis," *Clerestory:* "Mail Art," *Contemporary Voices from the Eastern World:* "Italics," *Drunken Boat:* "Provincial Hack" and "Oliphant and Castle," *Filling Station:* "Prelude to the End of this Book," "Attitudes and Non-Attitudes in May" and "The Journalist," *Five Fingers Review:* "Pasha Noise," *The Impercipient:* "The History of Wigging," *Onedit:* "In Pines," *Open City:* "Axis Thinking" and "Italics," *Premonitions: The Kaya Anthology of New North Asian American Poetry:* "Verl," *Rattapallax:* "Be Alive," *Shiny:* "We Make"

"No Special Order" and "Jai alai for Autocrats" appeared in the chapbook "Jai alai for Autocrats" published by Portable Press at Yo-yo Labs (New York).

"Thinning," "Poem Formerly Known as 'Terrorism'," and "They're Putting a New Door In" previously appeared in the chapbook "Poem Formerly Known as 'Terrorism'" and other poems" published by housepress (Calgary).

"Cull" appeared as a chapbook of that title, published by Tolling Elves press (London).

"Midas Ears," "Gatt Freedom," "General Statements Concerning the Rubberyard," "Corso," "I Had That Idea," "We Make," and "Howlings in Favor of Tulsa" appeared in a chapbook titled "The Window Ordered to Be Made" (A Rest Press, New York).

Parts of "What Does It Matter?" appeared in a chapbook "Pasha Noise: Life and Contacts" published by Oasis Press (Portland, Maine), on the web journal "MiPoesis," and on the Iowa Review website under the title "Coda: The Nineties Tried Your Game." The entire poem was published under its present title by Barque Press in England as a chapbook.

"Gatt Freedom" contains lines from Guy Maddin's "Death in Winnipeg," Guy Debord's screenplay "Howlings in Favor of De Sade" and "The Dullest Blog in the World" among other sources.

Grateful thanks to all of the editors of the above presses, journals and websites, especially: Derek Beaulieu, Andrew Brady, Thomas Evans, Brenda Ijima, Patrick Masterson, Ryan Murphy, Lyn Hejinian and Keston Sutherland. And to my friends.

Front cover photograph: "Tridax procumbens L" by Tim Davis
Author photograph: Rachel Szekely
Production Assistants: Octavia Davis, J.R. Osborn

What Is Said to the Poet Concerning Flowers, Brian Kim Stefans
First Edition, Factory School 2006
Heretical Texts: Volume 2, Number 4
Series Editor: Bill Marsh

ISBN 1-60001-048-2

factoryschool.org

Table of Contents

ৡ

for Rachel

What Is Said to the Poet Concerning Flowers

I AM WEDDED TO THE BUREAUCRACY

I am wedded to the bureaucracy
                     —these things have a way of sounding profound
     when you think about it
                 some of us do, tumultuously
but look up weirdly to find she has entered the room
                        lost
      not meaning to find you
         a retired martial arts expert now working for the government
of schenectady
       —today larry rivers died
         and now it's empurpled coffee for a half-dozen years
            of penance
—awesome idea
       though getting there was more interesting
     intimidating, enervating—I don't remember
                 but often had to go
to the bathroom when the theme of the approach got clearer
               and we got nearer
      to brooklyn—beginning to sing there, anxious of this or that
                       pausing by the concrete pools

THE REVOLUTION OF THE MIDDLE CLASS

The revolution of the middle class
                            will not be televised
        but preserved on caucasian
                                disks for millennia
in several hundred 96-page
                            books of limp poetry
            with titles right out of christian songbooks circa 1987
                                america
—we pledge allegiance to the
                            drag of tired instincts
                with victuals served up each night
                                    by bombers' wives in ashtrays
an entire calendar's worth of
                            metered doses and, of
        course, poetry advice columns
                            with assurance of bought votes,
of over-confidence—deep within the arbors
                                of perennial mature promise
            usurping the supplicant's one or two prayers
                                        reserved for our dispassionate guilt

IT'S POSSIBLY ABSOLUTE

It's possibly absolute
              —we are almost at the top of the rehearsal
    of stars—
        there is a lively one gone awol
to minnesota
          where several poets have died
       but only a few of them were named jack
                   canopy—
umbrellas are my favorite thing
            to balance on a dog with
       down sloping highways
              when the skyline is toward the east and
the hemlines
    —don't let me say that joke again
  I am almost in love with the privilege
             that brings your shy legs to me
in the simulacral hamptons
         —the shattered wrists of your economy
     wondering how this idiot got here
                 dearly holding his breath—for ardor

THE CROWDS WERE GETTING DRESSED

The crowds were getting dressed
                    after some communal nudity
      forced them to open the doors
                        to deserts of clothes
I had the teleprompter out
                    to influence the jury
          but there was very little getting by the fact
                            they couldn't read
—when nearly 7 feet of snow fell in 1957
                        language poetry was born
          in hauppauge
              just off route 96 (near the sunrise diner)—you couldn't have
anticipated the outcry then
                    even the dolphins were crying "intact"
      we had to arrest
                    several dozen for modal duplicity
being in love with the poem and in love with the weather
                            till nothing else mattered
      to them, to us, but to get on getting with it
                        robert creeley style, just beyond the sand "bar"

THE NEW CONSCIENCE IS LIKE THE OLD ONE

The new conscience is like the old one
                              only bluer
      with cool shark fins
                  —this video takes place in covert, west virginia
plans for the secession
                  are translated into swedish
          and left in a pile at an oblique angle
                              to the wind
—she was nearly
          seven months old when they named her
              "miana"
                        meaning *sedition-rose* in the native tongue
or *purse-on-a-string-*
                cutting-through-maudlin-ice-floes
      —I didn't talk to her much after that
                  and likened our chances of meeting to an asteroid's belt
tightening during a recession
                    —that couldn't have been too amusing
          and the über-kuhl soon returned to the suburbs
                        only to find the erotic quotient had all but dissipated

WE ARE PROBABLY VERY USED TO BEING ALIVE

We are probably very used to being alive
                              but getting started late
        is the fashion
                  —one almost tripped on his grandfather's birth—
and like cowards
              who refuse to write poetry, being
          indifferent, also, is an option
                            —that young slattern straight out of a
poem by william carlos williams
                        he proses all his visions in
              proposals for superior poses, which he adopts
                              dutifully
the first time she cleaved his straightened back and
                                the weather report went anal
      —who cares that the border between southampton and riverhead
                              is marked by shit
from a bipolar swan
                who mistook mattatuck for a bordello of baudelaire's
        geese—when it was really a parking
                          lot—we have our vulgar engines, so let's use them

This method is poetry
              pulling in "outside" feelings, habits, that wouldn't
     be acceptable
                   otherwise
but now like a toehold on to humanity's cliffs it
                                persists
          therefore you know my name
                            isn't the son of sam, isn't
stalin
          —in a related development there were those people that I once spoke to
               in a bar, New
                      Jersey, 1994, the one who
couldn't speak
          for the waves in his head
     being sanitized each day at
                    work—cleaning pools
royal comedy that would fail miserably on pay-per-view, and even
                                here
          where the method is poetry
                            keeping "outside" feelings, habits, strangely lusterless

ALL OVER THEORY MIGHT FIND IT'S WAY BACK

All over theory might find it's way back
                              out of the magazines, into the thistles
      and fires—bones and circumstance
                            —that was my retirement
plan
        to educate my laptop like a little blake child
          and bathe in the city
                            streets while I still had
my "build"
          —but this isn't august, and I've got a few things to say yet
                about life, and how I aim
                              to miss it
by spreading it thin like milk—by running the emotions, like data
                              through loops
      of saccharine, colorform hoops
                            —I noticed
they have a lot to do with the way we think these days, and I think
                                        that's fine
          but I do hope someday to get my plan off the ground
                              and—with the *possibility*—to win

The Window Ordered
To Be Made

ঽ

The Window Ordered
To Be Made

ॐ

To hospitalize the ones we love most
(Beginning an election and ending a corpse)
To take that money

I'm going to start on election day
(I'm basing this prayer on *Citizen Kane*)
I'm going to start
Asking the world if I'm straight
At a balloon lunge event, where lightness is fitness

Here (he shoved the aphrodisiac)
"Be in code!"
The Amish getting squeamish
(The net privileges
Transcendental Morse)
This essay is addressed to the audience
As I caught the misunderstanding of "fantail rout"

As I caught
That au courant
Autocrat hit the sky

So, talk through these sour depressions
And immigration counseling
We decided: we are a pair of absurdities
(I'm waiting for Scottish air)
Everyone thought you were beautiful
Now, to deliver the urban landscapes
Seems only normal: upsets, lapses, hosannas, bananas…

I am a happy
Victim of intelligence
(Robots picked up Willa at the airport)
"He probably went the wrong way with his eyes on"

Comedy?
Gene Wilder's an expert

These are like
Dropping off the guys off somewhere
(Bakunin's temp hair is limp)
The anonymity of the "I" on the web page
Remembers graduation
And the Chinese years symbolized by animals
Worthy of reading
If only for the erotica category
However badly spelt
By thirteen-year-old Petey Birdsong
(Within his mirrors of catoptromancy, etc. etc.)
Thirteen-year-old Petey Birdsong
(The rude mechanicals of *A Midsummer Night's Dream*)
Unbelievably endowed to play these sages
(Behind him, the walls were spread with the human body)
Thinking

Starting a Gore
And ending a wimp

                              bluish

Can burn this

                    with this kind of information
                    available to panic

The Journalist

"My body is a roulette wheel, and I am betting on red."
—Aragon

૨

One man reported that his computer
"appeared to have been hacked by a redhead,
and she sang to herself while doing it."

Another conveyed his position on recent developments
in Van Halen: he was an "anti-Samite."
I want to be immune again.

*

He paws his own body. This is the violence
of wisdom.

*

But like we don't remember the day we were born,
no one ever thinks about the first letter of a sentence
with *fondness.*

*

Yap yap yap yap yap—ambient poetics.

They're Putting A New Door In

ৡ

Brian's new shoes. She asked me of his whereabouts. They're putting a new door in.

CCI. They're putting a new door in. Impersonating an officer.

They're putting a new door in. Feliz Navidada. My watch continues to stop: self-identity.

> I break,
> WFMU.
> Margin time,
> the steaming metropolis
> wakes
> at 8 am
> with dry lips.
> I couldn't take my eyes off the ball.

Papers on her head. Like a crown of spring thorns. They're putting a new door in.

This is only the third poem I've written in 2001. And probably the last one. The other two went like this:

> It hit with the farce of an atom bomb.
>
> If there are no animals on Mars, is there anything that could classify as "shit."
>
> People are like ciphers. They say this, they say that.
>
> Private life is a social experiment.
>
> The French: an impatience with secular explanations.
>
> Writing. Boiling potatoes.
>
> Everybody's pride is hurt.

And:

> Footfalls, bubble baths,
> Hezbollah and hot dogs.
> Be sure to add these Tones of War
> to your arsenal of meters.

Howlings in Favor of Tulsa

ঽ

He learned the seven *Gracias*
in the Countess Second's
flat. The reality principle changed the face
of religious discipline: tossed up girls

with Aquinas buttocks.
Afterwards,
spilled cosmos made patterns
of roses in the pool. Raoul Vaneigem

ended up on one of those Iraqi playing cards.
To be free,
and ice skating! marvel of the furry
caterpillar scooting across

fragrant, come-and-get-em lawns.
We are saddened.
Communist floes icened
his face. Our country pays Puritanism

to heave out doubt.
We are the floridas of Tulsa,
but we are the cavities of the Future!

General Statements Concerning the Rubberyard

ॐ

General blankets descend on the rubberyard.

This pistol holistic
piles in the whinny
of the rubberyard. The dorsal trope
adjusts the rubberyard, until
stentorian, "profound."
Germinal sweetness in the rubberyard.

Cocks crow to bay their respects to the rubberyard.

For sale:
fat, and a glucose thermometer.
Mom will come out to widen the toes
teased into renaissance.
There tends to be win doughs there.
Fleece can succumb to viscous aspects.
Lars von Trier vamps like a condor
                                        in the rubberyard.

Halliburton pinched a nipple in the rubberyard.

Why think of the rubberyard? Ambulance

photograph of the rubberyard, while

moving only, the cotton strokes
of color against agate blue skies leveling
the barns, mares, trowels
of the rubberyard, in white, stand-offish light

collected in a book on a table in Williamsburg, VA.
The seventy presidents of the rubberyard tinkle.
The wives of the rubberyard presidents tinkle severely.
Oh, green holiday spirits!

Stained-
glass windows keep the descendents

unhappy, but productive in masses.
A boat blocks the wham from unhappening.
Treacly fellows with gnashing bangs
deploy the ferns to the vernacular quizzes.
Of an "ooh" and an "ohh" we know nothing
but numbers. Numbers of sales from the rubberyard.

When the movie is rotunda
I could not wish a crimp, sure and sulfite-free
or a lathe bourbon, sloppy
purred by a hipster in orange condoms.

Stench of the frolic still lingering—like a fence!—by her eyes.

Corso

২

Self-hatred: keeping your arms spread out.

The Crocodile Honey elopes
in carat-clusters   pixilated zoom control makes it Marden-like
I'm happy to have masked my   self-hatred
These are first tests   of the new morn.
          pip of fire alarm   duct-taped to top of
alabaster bust of penguin.
This is a rudimentary happenstance   on letterhead titled "Corso."
I've melted in a wee bonnet
                holding your small hand in
mine
          You were like three small pieces of asparagus, then.

But the relationship lasted.
We've witnessed other mornings like this
          new one.
And you can't say: "Stop."

And you can't follow after my mother like you lean to.

Prelude To The End Of This Book

ঽ

Here we are, sunning in mutual esteem.
You are one head higher, and my jaw
is a chisel. Can / I / Point / Blank.

They are revolving like tops around us,
in silence and a credit to the music.
Paths / Furious. Nothing to fear, nothing
to abut: a scene as orchestrated
      as the parroting of complex clauses.

What waxes is my memory,
and wanes my attention.
      Ellipses and eclipses, the constant in such situations;
to create a situation becomes my only cause,
secure defeat. Treated / You / Blind.

And more powerful, contributing
to the conversation, the clipped
pitch and prick of French classical
prose: alive, at last.
      Humming vocoder effect
from the kitchen; more wine founds
the tabula rasas. Clumsy gallants stumble amidships.
Stereo / Crime / Philosophy / Achievement.

As the knowledge production moves along
humbly,
recordings of whales. No / Future.

The creations of the newspaper collagists
are whistling through the alleys of dearth.
One death among many; talents have their names.
Ambition gestures career
      through California night sky.

Water / For / Dunes. I will suffer
the maxims while you stuff lead. My sex
for community
      and your wealth
for self;

participants are sequestered until self-esteem
acquires capital seduction. Piano sound wells
from the bedroom. This is our Song, jean-commercial style.

Finally, the embarrassment over smoking
offers way out: fancy wounds
are cerebral. Some myth or rhythm;
finally, giving that up.
                        Tick / Tick / Tick / Haunted.

Move to Brazil. Something like Pink Floyd
atmospherics; something decades-past
achieves new relevance. Peek-a-boo eyes
like steady-cams in the toilet swilling darkness: lost.

At the end of the game they alphabetize the names.

Count yours in it.

Too / Tall / Harry.

One / With / Sun / Stick.

Instrumental break will not convert them;
she races through the galleries, gender-crippled.
Hostile arrangements:
                        it's called editing.

The plug. Smooth issue. Some subtle subtext
is like hard rock candy at center of Jupiter;
thesis uncovers it. Target it:
your back.
Sensible writing on the causes of
                        Twentieth-century clinamens.

The word's out: cut your mouth. Bargain in the park.
I should just rip up those poems and create prose narratives
out of them, like I'm doing
now. It's now coming back,
with conversation about social leperdom
                        in 1952. Lucked / Bird / Perspective.

Not enough crescendo
                        in that lazy throat;
the tongue keeps the car waxed in the garage.

Scholarship redeems him.
Anchorites "know" all the restaurants.

Play-by-plague calling; anything goes
in the deleting delirium of raising the kids
in hell. Black / Coo / Retina.

You can stop it; left hand is the *writer.*
The fiercest accuser claims that I'm ungenerous;
the freedom fighter exonerates elitism;
soon, an anthology is considered:
                              popguns.

Given any time, and the web of incestuous comeuppance
generates its angular rose.
Vocal / Caverns.

Piece by piece, toward Calgary. Sonnets
of thunder; chapbooks of grease.
Split along binaries, the mind—no chance—
flicking among such bodily perspectives.
Remember that. Dollars and sense
                    will look good in your font.

Notebooks that reveal.
Why can't I find love when so many cathedrals
profess detail to the pedestrian?
                    And the mawpy-jawed of
us
become significant antennae.
Among life and contacts: technology.

Formerly / Known / As /

Prince.
Dropping a scene into the non-linear prestidigitator;
nine resolutions to potential catastrophe
of numbing, libidinal catharsis.
                    One / Catalyzed / Them.
In bobby-sox and tennis shoes, nothing else.

The vexed poetics of Sunday morning news host;
pass the finger foods because nothing else matters;
sensation provides ballast of the future in icicles
of light; piano wells. You are taller. We talk about basketball.

Attitudes And Non-Attitudes In May

ৡ

1.
You can see the clarity in Philby's thinking in how few corrections he's made.

2.
You will face the *Luftwaffe*—alone.

3.
Striving to be insulted:
it's like the reality principle:
a kind of receiving station
for the ephemera of daily trust.

4.
(They were pointing us toward their absolutes.)

5.
Those questions that have caused you so much anxiety
do not have to be answered.

6.
Any life is tainted.
Hence, no touching the fleshy, lubricated parts.

7.
Gottfried Benn observing the flower of a fatal knife wound.

8.
Walking away with the sunlight on your shirt.

Provincial Hack

ৡ

1.
I would like to expand my sphere of influence
        to include gummy bears, flutes, and broken raisins.
(A cloud
        at sunset.)

2.
So torque, avoid the quack
        bitching in the room you're with.
Um, sending…
        (Blending in).

3.
"Everybody steals.
        It is exciting."
No symbols are involved…
        You cannot drink annotated water.

4.
Tiny bubbles in the soap…
        Like condoms…
Tiny zeroes in the astroturf…
        (The telephone hangs up of its own course.)

5.
The Kim Stefans sneak attack is now in progress.
        Be not upset.
(Just velvety and dark
        slashes and dreams.)

6.
It's all musicals.
        Youth culture in zip-locks.
Here is the colon:
        and here, its Happy Meal™.

7.
Maybe this is what they mean by television:
        Brion Gysin's ginny flix… bottom-up bureaucracy…

Tracing lies against the pattern
        in mystic squalls, conveying them.

8.
A sort
        of syndrome.
Natural, of course.
        (California.)

9.
To complain of no love
        and then to make movies.
(Drifting into minis,
        a chorus of NAFTA girls.)

10.
With the largest of handshakes keeping us sound
        again and again... returning to the same apartment...
Cool, gov!
        "Eye warrant."

11.
Spilling out toward the coasts in sex drives,
        every one of them (the coasts, that is).
Little stickers on the ceiling
        some gnarly, be-acned kid put there...

12.
or her, maybe.
        You consider Nicaragua
the imagination.
        (Pork chops and apple sauce.)

13.
"I'll be dead soon."
        Boo hoo hoo.
Sane as myth, he renewed his function with eloquence:
        writing *Tarantula* over and over again.

14.
In those filthy Thirties...
        the low-res screen capture habit...
the Cancer League Aggression Party...
        the Gabriela Sabatini Intelligence Project...

15.
Mein Gott!
       (Pauses.)
"One doesn't sense a personality so much
       as a *strategist*." I could almost write a poem about it.

16.
Meaning: "*Just* a poem…"

A Poem for Tyros

২

Apollinaire,
argue with,
art binary breakdown
—but enough to derail,
—but I'm in a rush.

Chance,
come into play,
comes out of his/her mouth,
concentration on the words on the table.

Consider my very private
constant movement,
Debord—
I am the system,
I can't say
I am not,
if only slightly.

I walk into a room.
I would do it in improvised locations.
I'll spare the examples.
I've wanted to create a paragraph
walking a lobster
walking into a room.
It's not that I'm uncomfortable
meeting people
perhaps at odd moments of the month and week,
perhaps on purpose.

Nuances
of the bureaucratic—
of written text into the real-time
"on schedule,"
one among many.
Perhaps *dictator* is better?
Perhaps a series of paragraphs?

The bodily/abstract (

The public/private (
The troubles,
The written stuff
—there is a page of wasted prose.
There is no exact.

Well,
what else happens at a reading?
When the time seems right (

You become the "boy," and those who have nurtured private opinions of your essential ser-
        vility suddenly come forth with demands—
through thick or thin,
to be gazed at as a single artwork—
not to mention potentially transform thinking in fashions that writing itself could not alone
        do—
they are just demands—
they are mostly petty,
(think of Bourdieu)
which is to say that the most loyal curators will never be taken too seriously as poets.

A "gentleman," but really a slave)—
a certain looseness,
as did the behavior of Rimbaud,
as he/she does,
a poet's actions in public (
a series hanging in space at the same time.

Can one say "being" of the work that you have produced,
—determined warrior-poet who has attempted to inflict on me the natural aspect of the
        superiority of his views but who has not
become part of the record?—
becomes animated for me?
And when they have just produced some tremendous work that I am sure will change
        everything,
even organizing,
even the use of proper names,
ever so slightly,
for instance,
for the possible in what,
for what,
for whom decisions have a sort of finality—
I somehow think this is all meaningful.

I think it is discussing this particular strand of my behavior

—I try to shave at least in the week prior to the reading—
I have just completed a two-month run as the "curator,"
—even approached mastery of the social rules such that such a challenge could even be
          humored past the first move,
in fact.

And if it weren't so much work—
and only with poets I am most excited about—
and quite alone—
and so for that reason I will "curate" only infrequently.

Promises:
quasi-elitist self-training as a poet
—setting the parameters,
since it is then,
so much more revealing in my writing,
syntax even—
talker—
that a particular aspect of poetry
that begin with this sentence
that is lacking in the creation of a "schedule"
not to mention my own social distractions
of cultural capital
will be my expression of revolutionary will,
writer,
yes.

All of the vicissitudes (
and I promised to myself that spontaneity,
accidentally or purposely ignore,
actually enjoy the microphone,
inchoate as it seems.
including reviewer,
interpretation,
issues of mutual respect,
—it is the French who have most theorized how the agent in the field
invariably makes an impression on Nerval's works (
playing in a super-literary fashion invariably changes not only what has been written

but the trap of filling a role—

But then I am reminded that this form of politics smacks.
But what is to be written?
by chance (
etc.

These run up against these more *fluid* inclinations of mine,
(this is a key word here)
this *visibility* is good—
though I have sought to master it by pulling some of the *strings*—
—that you take *orders*,
—that you are perfectly *polite* (
the "iron hot," if that doesn't sound *ridiculous*.

And I would have thought I'd have gone out of my way to avoid the "public" as much as
        possible,
and though I have no terribly urgent thoughts on the matter,
how many idiotic challenges have I faced from a headstrong
I am not just in the system.
I am political just when I said that being political is the natural next step past being an aesthete.
?
In which I can most suitably begin a sentence:
"Three-dimensional world are often thwarted by a haughty attitude toward the rules them-
        selves...

To read in private—
whom I might chance to meet?
More so now than in the headier days of life/
that which one is intended.

That you behave in fashions that suit your role?
These opportunities for continuing the discourse—
(why can't I spell that?)
agreed-upon term for this role in the poetry community—
but it doesn't have the prestige of that figure in the visual arts.
But it somehow becomes a determinant in the reception.

Oliphant And Castle

ঽ

Someone was fat and happy.
       (I've learned to write
on the marble.)
Does it pay to care about things?
       One could be precocious
and start a Day Op,
(first, we'd have to know what that is
and stop caring about being lonely)
       —did you forget her conversation
so quickly, because
you were drunk for days afterwards?
       Hopping on tiny leather springs.

No Special Order
(no soap, no taters, no government)

ৰ

1.
And so the old new order and the new old order
have called my bluff: I don't have moods
clinging to the cot—for pretty much the entire match
squirting eighty percent of the style,

there were fractions of a name, bar/café doggerel
with signals influenza'd by historical speech, but
statistically unkempt, a spastic honesty
in twelves. Didn't think about it a lot, just wrote

becoming the tradition, massive in someone's
delinquency, leashed to the inquisitive
and howling. Like you, I lied, tried to make it
a book—capsized by life, but only for the century.

    Feet were hung, and for an instant
    my passions sprang from a gaudy intent.

2.
As the cat whined over the fans, as the critical lore reminded
me of the past, approaching like pews, and of
the precious order of salmon fugues
I found I could surf—martial arts imperatives

from community opacity—hike like pines the splits, plume
day-glo colored, like a Brat in a Hat,
climb back into the trapezoids and bull circuits
shimmering Today, yet falsely accused

on schedule—irreverence dosing the regularity
flaring from the coverts, vicious. One more big-breasted
star, godforsaken, in doubt control,
professing obedience to sound, though amateur at love.

    The engineers could fake their cues
    and strike hot dials, but no one is disabused.

3.
In fact, they ignored this shagadelic approach.
Greening the technique, and finally surfacing,
now "massive in someone's delinquency," *their* drums became
the quatrain, incensed quarantine, so what

sound choked untold in the Thirty States, in robust
naming technique, citizens arranged
to marble in fountains of sleepovers, for the market in bleeps
and poses—then croons then screams—and so

they sleep. Why make a cancer of it? you
ask, waving the anti-depressant book, stalking the oat of
the boy in undevious health, in pregnant
vessels, variety ever squandered, penitents sharpening their knives,

      spurious? Fashions, wisps of hair.
      Dull, domestic sounds that flake the air.

4.
I don't have moods, though am particularly alive
in my distractions, doing the taste test
on this or that, mixing demure and fickle conventions
with the protectful and shy, with a signature

muddy celerity, demonstrating a crick
in the conscience—if only while 24-hour sunrise permits
shitting in the pants for kicks. I won't write
what it is that embarrasses me, not *that*

nirvana, even with opportune chagrin—before, that is, awakening,
final, approved, immaculate,
with all the tragedies of the world in my marsupial
pouch. Nothing squandered, and to a furious passion

      in liege. And in leisure, possessed.
      Dispossessed I mean, my truth the rest.

Midas Ears

ই

"We" have found roses cheaper than cigarettes.

(Putting a square patch on your shoulder to kill an *instinct*.)

Perhaps
I will stay here, away from your writing

divided between the rout of Pollocks
and What's Said to the Poet Concerning Flowers.

*

I stop,
and wave.
Then punk happened.

Cull

ঽ

QUIET

It's so quiet I can hear the Kurds.

IN A STATION OF THE METRO

Ended
During a movie.

Of Bodies

These are my clothes.
I organize them like stars.

New York

; participants are sequestered until self-esteem acquires capital seduction.

*

This is our Song, jean-commercial style.

MINIATURE (ORKNEY LYRIC)

My mother with the half moon eyes
(oh! she's had a bit to drink,
her eyes are usually minus signs).

DO YOU THINK THERE HAS BEEN A BRAIN DRAIN FROM RUSSIA TO THE WEST

It takes a lot of brains to create a drain in Russia.

PIFFLE.

(Breath.)

Man can take time to believe this.

THE FAT THAT BUNCHED UNDER HER CHIN

I will never get over it.

Horn

like trying to fill a cow
with thimblefuls of milk

At The Edge Of Wilderness

Sean's boobs.
What would you do, just lay there and let it happen?

FOR W.S. GRAHAM

I am still. And I hear the words
are still, also, but I can't tell.

GO NOW

You have been named Synonymous
So dance like a monkey.

Thinning

ঽ

An ethic node
Facewidth

Protecting toxic parts
Waxy

If I see this dog
Lady + 3

Have some lynch
Officer

To guilt
Things for complex rooms

Australian rules
Summer

Available thinking
Hopes to dog

Strong
Visiting

You know the miracle
Club

Then enjoy it
Clown

Honestly
When 4 and 6 forewarned

Spiderglass
Creations

Poem Formerly Known
as "Terrorism"

ৱ

The feng shui was glistening.
(This helps me to avoid the air of polemic.)
I am like you
At ten.
Might that be your swimming?
Medically, in a division game
("Squid" revealed to be floating cheese)
A low-res boyfriend
(He talked about them like they were hotrods)
Two
In a decade
Who could scan the headlines, but who could say
Who'd laugh.
Go rent a video on it.

"Capture"
The track ball.
You are gorgeous
In information silence.
We are in a "wracked" dominion.
(I trust
The slow writer.)

"Green tortoise-shell glasses" is not an adequate response.

"Islamabad" is not an adequate response.

So that   I could have a switch
In blue motion.
Visitors: a talcum blonde, Jihad vs.
McWorld
(To relate to the anecdote:
It is just struggling to find a form
To our kids.)
So I motion:
The Pentagon, symbol of our erotic hope.
How much are we really paying attention to ourselves?

In quiet times, like these
Censored apparitions
(Our fog there)
I'm hurt like Rocky
(Time to replace something
In 1939). Is it my gallant?
In 1939.
There she is   doing that Munch thing again.
Sad, anemic eyes
Coming to take the piss   out of you.

"Spontaneous creation"
Their own sort
Of sound poetry.
(You wasting   you time.)
Anyone who has ear glasses
Amid Third World Revolution
Renewals.
His famous Mom.
(These weren't opposites   somewhere.)
Mary had a jab.
Like hell you didn't know.

IwyuriuCu '0 oiu woiuC uaf wX oide l'Tu
Ewyuwau rdnn.   Cutud.u oide
Lwuyb nuo yu euu
        —dX t'aLo ln'h rdoi ou!
EdTa'ne?
,

Sdob 'af 'nouC oiu yue'Tu do twao'dauec—
When does the world open up and become true?

This functioning   as a numchuck
Pug pouring filth
(Ping chocolate)
Rendezvous   of course.
Maine: I heard it myself, now thinking this.
Pedantic.
Showering with all his glee
("Last call for the Devonshire armpit!")
On the grounds of
Tables.
Repopulated Paris
("They won't understand this.")
Catholic dances.

Paris, henceforth, will want to be repopulated.

Versus the hurricane.

A wasted effort   you have said nothing.
Jack Nicholson
Relaxes
In disco tempo
Thursday morning
Begins to create live sets.
From the ego-sphinx, Matrix-like, you jump.

Hanging.

All the computers whisper: *acqui, acqui.*
They didn't hand out
Spinach.
(I'm going to remind them.)
Twelve easy precipices
Going out
Cold solids   (we're stuck with his company
Now).
(Talk whizzes by like hands
Pushing the computer.)
I fresh toothen up   bucky balls   graffiti on "lunge."

—The Blue Upset.
—Upset in Blue.
—A deep and fascinating
Distrust
Section in Synthetic Scots.
And after that: the shopping.

One doesn't "sense" a personality
A dial of Genet's girls
The adult.
Conic section   avant-gardists
How many people
Live life at
Glibbest
(You said that
Benny Hill.)   Just the same
Field of glory.   Thighs of the apple tree.

Ritual
Natural expressions.
Wildcarpets.   (Novel or criticism
Same thing.)
Beneath the razor.
Beneath your hands.
69

Twenty seconds later:
Isolated mountain
Singing fits
A noticeable humor in the climate
Off the roof
In which your loves circulate
Greek.
Everything is useful!
Against this genius!
I met her at the United Artists   Theater on Broadway

People with nice teeth being perfectly superficial

In "patois"

To save money.

Gatt Freedom

ৱ

Mailbomb: I had a mug of coffee sitting on my desk.
Mantis: I reached out my hand and picked up the mug.
Market: I had several pieces of paper in front of me.

Reaction:
I suddenly began to hate the Specialist
  wild and white choreography unleashed
on a semiotics-ignorant public—
   None of them love you.
   Happiness is a new idea.

The fine young artificial
  proto-mullets are so natural
brazen vessels, buttery-soft.
  I continued to sit there for a while.
It was a terrifying and grotesque site,
   but the Specialist continued:
   "Say, did you sleep with Francoise?"

   None of them love you.
   Happiness is a new idea.

Playboy: The lace on one of my shoes was undone.
Plutonium: I depressed the switch on the side of the kettle.
Plutonium: I continued to sit there for a while.

Pseudonyms:
  "Just as the film was about to start, Guy-Ernest Debord would climb on
  stage to say a few words by way of introduction. He'd say simply:
  'There's no film. Cinema is dead. There can't be film any more. If you
  want, let's have a discussion'."

Data-haven,
  the counterfeit siblings
(William Gates)
  covert video:

so natural
  I'm no longer self-conscious

using my hand
>when the convulsions had subsided.

Buddhistic and bland
>*(Journey to the Moon)*
in the cafés
>of Saint-Germain-des-Prés!

their revolts become
>conformisms. Twenty-one
years: at that age,
>one is capable of all acts of civil life.

>*When*
>>*the number is*
>>>*over—*

I continued to be apathetic with my activities.

Reflections in a Glass House

ঽ

AAA Another American Artist   —each axis
spawns another axis—   And—and?
        a sort of beggar's testament—typed
that's not me—   —whom I know you might
consider one of the lightweight artist-intellectuals of our time—
    perhaps not the most productive)   —or espe-
cially—   Did the flounder flounder—the bass
bass?   as I am also dissatisfied—
    in London town—   —you have to live
with it—practicing in Brooklyn—   Finessing
the first kiss.   For your pleasure—try the
Mount Rushmore posture for any longer than 15 years—
    Seconds ago—   —poverty—abjection—
        —named her—   with the sky just
pissing over the horizon.   —the lad's skinny
legs barely activated for the days ahead, the eyes still red from summer's
lawn chairs—   Hello hello.
    I was lying.   —it was nearly voted in
—the amendments constructed   —and the toxic verticality of
its filaments integrated into the country's fabric—
as the moment is digital—   —unbothered—
        —axis thinking—   like nation ⇔ indi-
vidual   —real people—real poems—
        Well—I thank you—   It doesn't
pay to be conservative.

•

it is anti-Wagnerian—in this sense—   It opens.
    Let me warn you: Lust never troubled me.
Maybe tomorrow.   —and the color's flawed—
        —so playing tennis won't solve much of anything
    —neither his own nor   My lazy glands will
ever support me.   My sense is that one can find
an analogy in poetry   Nation is easily
placed on the axis of transnation ⇔ nation   —
a headache in a ballroom   —constant—

—the trade of all sophists—   —
slow tones that surrender themselves finally—in the mist—
    Or hell   —certainly when—
    "watch me getting fucked every which way" the thin hair of our informa-
tion   Professionals.
Politesse with the finger bent.   be simply a diagram
for memory—   —you can replace it if you'd
like—   Fisher-Price joys now that the idea of
the flood has subsided.

●

—so—then—yeah—   description
        falters   —they'll never get
anywhere—   —speaking among them-
selves with polysyllabic cardinals and heliocentric ordinals
    pull the elastic back   before such robust
confusion   More creativity lugged through weasel
holes.   not tired—
governs the lack   —though with respect—
        So few—   So said those Pop
dudes.

●

Some of this screaming from Tan Dun seems to reflect this impassiveness—
                cathartic but recorded—
Bob Mould—in Cleveland—insensate.   —
bad gums—   Stamping.
    Standing in the zone.   —lyrical—in
expanded volumes; this scum records dutifully the you of us and should live.
                Surprise!   —
perhaps—   *speaking—worth nothing.*
    jimmy the lock—vandalize the key—   —
don't sing what is well made by Irish—   —
retract everything   —words don't know these
physical boundaries—   —as Duchamp
famously quipped   "dataflow—"
    not to anticipate a later critical attitude toward the finished work so much
as to maintain the aura (or era) of exploration   —
you will have no success   —so Providence
awaits   global cellular rates—

the number of croutons baking away—
bruiser   some complicated punctuation
          —some embryonic female who could make sense of all this.
          Of course!   *Tom Stinkmetal is man.*
               Too Much Entropy?
DVD—with a razor and beer—   —
screamed Calibanic fortune-cookies at Studio 54—
—unawares of our zeitgeisty question looming like Woody Allen's brassiere
over the fields with a *slurp-slurpy* sound (special effects);
—though—   kemosabee
     —like some presidential candidate   —the
beach delivered the body of Malcolm X   —
waltzing so softly   —this action
   —to be skies edible as text daily to determine it—
relax   —so long as you are aspiring to love
          —but as love is inspiring the atmosphere
   —we've turned a corner   Usually—
          borders of Dumbo—   Very fine—
thank you.   Very fine—thank you.
   —flowing down in predictable cascades for all to see—
   set out for them   With a million
things to remember—   Wanking—the boy
returned to his home not crying   larger defi-
nition   healthy breakfast merely that—
          and given an "Asian mom" perm.   —
there clomb a tree

●

barely able to lift the chin   —that teething
          We are both conformists if I understand you correctly.
          though it sounded like French soufflé fed through a Kaos box—
               The dullness receding—
the gritty matter; to deposit this egg in a brown bag on the reader's
doorstep—   —I don't know how to
   the "realms" and one more sure argument for literacy amongst those who
don't know—   Weeping consolations.
          —cross-legged—   —ratted-on
products—   —quality of printed production—etc.
          When writing—making the fishbowls round.

I Had That Idea

ৠ

I had that idea, too.

Write the life but according
to principles not usually associated
with life, such as…

And shut off all
auto-correct features.

There is the sound of straining
from the other room. That was the one
vacated by the Terrorists. They were brothers
from a little village in Italy. It is now

occupied by an opera singer
with chronic constipation.

Same thing. Taking the pleasure
out of your work.

I had serious reservations
about my own writing before I started
this. This talking.

Sometimes it is just
the hands hanging from twin flagpoles
emanating from my breasts. I could shine them,
wax them, spit on them, but they don't

write, just hold out for the rest of the day
until I couldn't brag of them any
longer—usually by mid-afternoon, say 3 pm.

I'd drink more coffee then, check my emails,
play some on-line *Yahoo!* games, like backgammon.
My flagpoles not buckling in the wind.

My flags empty of wind.
My hands dangling there like flags.

What Does It Matter?
or, Pasha Noise: life and contacts

A sort of fiction

"For the Law kills the flesh that kills the Law,
And we are then alive."
—E. A. Robinson, "The Three Taverns"

"Subjectively."
—Ezra Pound, "Hugh Selwyn Mauberley"

What Does It Matter?

২

1. OVERTURE: BIRTH AND DEBATES

The idea of a programmer's pride, pulled from a kid's acrimony;
they had codified it into torques, fixtures
insular debates and demographic fissures;
prophylactic explanations culled from bells and whistles
colorful, synaesthetic, could lead the way
from Sunday school antics to enviable paychecks;
but that radical parity slumped in the punk of a groin,
so that, later, what made ties to the critical
olfactory nerve as it hovered over New York
were the generations of teethers we saw entering the debates;
a dark humor obtained, a cyber-sexual,
middle-aged vaudeville of what was relentless, though it seemed to fly away
the moment the game got hot, and Pasha
settled into his mitts, telling them Style was enough—no positions
necessary—they'd been obviated by the reticular clown.

2. OVERTURE (2)

A visit to the world's largest tenement phone;
beep-bop in the schism of necessity
frees up nothing but an attic room for history;
his ratings plummeted shortly after that,
accusations swell, dull Caliban's lashes,
with marches in the streets against the evitable classes;
the paterfamilias balloon swooped overhead, then
swung down over the table, shouting
"Good disciple!" and "Pardon my Canadian French!"
later to be bullied by the falcons, ravens, owls;
now that we know how wonderful the 21st century
can't be, waking up isn't difficult anymore,
the pen—or stylus, rather—leaps gingerly into the hand,
or cyborg claw, a synaptically-enhanced lockjaw
since our inadequacies turned out not to be fiction after all.

3. MODERN LOVE

Flipping slap-happy from one purple pose to another;
the techno-fusion drones, some dehydrating drug
tames it—one argot-like name exchanged for "schizophrenic" Other;
she, though, had eyes for an audience,
had acquired the moniker Her Videoness Avatar, in a dream
—she's clumsy on manic ankles, rewriting Beckett;
the avenue was suggesting Pasha, and with focus he arrived,
out of the blue, subjectively—dubious, barely audible
over the crackle of World War II headphones, mincing slogans
cryptic and fueled, and very faux-Latinate;
when they finally marry, HVA and Pasha, they are near-dead, or
le mot juste might be, for the canon, "reptilian"
—cold, unblooded, but they nonetheless spark a friendship
through email, in the humid, bull days of August,
and one day decide to visit the Brooklyn Botanical Gardens.

4. Modern love (2)

One more sally;
rock song strums
and calms the nerves;
they shop,
privately interact
with thumbs;
the processor whirs
commandments overhead,
now uttered
with certainty;
real playstation
or organic whist,
serotonin
straddles the DNA
one last time for thought.

5. Planet telex

Telex squandered his chance for fame, crying What are my interests;
multiple piercings suggest a fractal physiology, not
of the skin, but of the heart;
late nights, tattooed to a bar stool, leashed
to a portable assistant, vigilant in this fiction—sometimes
striking upward, out, for a gust of air, nagging about Empire;
such vision flicks us
haplessly into a void that was shimmering Testicle Beauty,
—proses of diamonds, he said, somnolent but serenaded by liquors, he
said—potable dream assailant from the past;
our vagueness is mint, remarkable, a
culture can thrive on it: virgin splash pages and IPOs for the masses
offered instead of names, concepts, symbols and
words, figures, lines, stories, and
of the rest of this matter, one purrs into the receiver, and expectorates.

6. Heat death

The syntax will appeal to the women, the words will appeal to the men;
green, yellow, red, these variations can cause an accident
extending the highways back into the Meadowlands;
what fickle remains of a once confident transportation,
some outside source will remark, concluding the system's fucked,
then decrying the self-animation of stained glass;
but Olive Oil still says: "I'm taking the brat to the country,"
the sun reflecting arrows on fields of vintage wheat,
and until her face slips off into her glass, she is famously believed,
the house turning stone silent after that;
but when the tea leaves are read, and Bartelby eclipses his spreadsheets,
a population will suggest itself in several violet languages
true to a will, though still bartering with Pokemon cards—speaking
a language that, in time, is to be praised for its efficiency
and, given the proper addictions, will probably support a new literature.

7. Heat death (2)

Because the quality was Miguel in the bone shop of visions;
the destiny was Marianne, that parody was dozens
plinking on silver planes the future of American cinema;
we require a touch of the arbitrary in our quest for preternatural solace,
also, a moment of tossing, vertiginous sex action
why not, among the sonnet-like insubstance of the screenplays;
a damsel in distrust and a hero's piezoelectric bladder,
the villagers rebel, soundman farts on ladder,
this all faithfully scripted by the blind, teenage amanuensis
unionized since daybreak, but sweating in plastic running pants;
finally, the expected demise wings into focus, the
suspicions of Prym the gardener metamorphose into social contraband,
lovers bathe in the shade of a milk-white Vaseline filter
long-banished by the Nouveau Roman people but who, finally, cares,
this program has its meanings and afterwards there's no story, but laughter.

8. HEAT DEATH (3)

It is in the depths of this rhetoric that the hidden quantity persists;
a jujube, a scar, a dandelion, all are permitted to obtain
the paradigm that is a counter-thrust to the hypocrisy;
what stories he had told when reclining deep in his deathbed,
she said, but said she couldn't remember them, yet
that Saturday ceased to impress with its abysses of unsolved fairness;
and so the stories survive beyond the pale light
of ideology, philosophy, language even, and the attractive trends, acquiring
for themselves the aura of rare, sought-out fashions
so that the codgers were revived, to resist, but that was all wrong;
what was right was the inviting darkness
in the confusions of cellular syntax and vocabularies culled from dream musics,
the voices coalescing and retarding, vexing but never bland,
leveled against each other in the no-holds-barred of a facile, bitstream rhetoric,
—such that, with hindsight, one notices a slight scar on the shoulder.

9. DAY JOB

Crammed in a rectangle;
the concentration
is on the warp on the floors;
words loaned
by knowing smiles
and *every single breeze*;
the scrotum
a tight pack or frowning,
calligraphic twists
marl Hokusai's garden;
so earnest,
few could he call his friends,
but mother, hearing,
and sound, his father,
tell-tale whistle from the throat.

10. ARTIFICIAL PARADISES

We observed the star fields;
no concern they were artificial,
some dream-bot of adolescents;
make that *overpayed* adolescents,
they tolerate my shoes, and
their fishy way of love-making;
this aristocratic disinterest,
something to do with words,
indelible words, on a typewriter, by
a hand that is seamless blood;
an economy for the taking, one's
health derides the ease of it,
blank slate chalked by fascist disco
drone—cathexis by Tourette's,
until the fancy trance repays the work.

11. Q & A

All that time, all that easy time;
frozen in mannered applause,
a country of hunches waits;
there, by the military therapy monitors,
the Byzantine conversations,
the dissociative stares, the passing off;
for Pasha, like them, it was nothing
but a game, his flint flecks of culture
comporting in easy tournament
with light sabers, in polyvinyl memory "aids";
digital caffeines, he said, tangible
placebos to palliate the feeble-martyred
—Tepid E-zine was on a roll now, too, so
they, allies at university conferences,
returned to dust: the funded, the dispossessed.

12. WILLIAMSBURG

If society were an opinion, you'd be lying;
the brain is lighter without eating,
but the lines of poetry all scintillant mistakes;
"retention theory"—we smoke them out until
apotheosis in the critical sublime, still practiced
here, in New York—no need for a socializing ardor;
in Britain, they are fixing for order, not
of the American sort, with sorties occurring regularly, but
as counterpoints, with their justifications uncovered
in the Empire's darker, debt-laden lashes;
a towering, Britney-Spearsish blonde looks on
from the billboard outside my window—I think, to remind
me... of... not sure... blankness... or
that it's not the "Nineties" anymore (or not for ninety more years)
—the walls and curbs an integrated, influential sphere.

13. DIVORCED

"And then I start getting this feeling of exaltation";
but that's before the brass Daddy-arm
unscrews from the pewter socket;
Telex monitored the weight of potential catastrophes
from the gorse-like foliage of his apartment,
unstandard, victimized, divorced;
but that was like the sentience of carved, Mayan statues
exporting their carnal desires in dissipated "men's" magazines,
rewiring the mores to reflect how unstrange
this is—futuristic, chic, enveloped;
smacking bubble sounds from the packing gels used for storage
of Panama potatoes, rerouted through Greece,
with the English wines of substance control kept driftily at bay,
far from the ops of hummers, anti-aliased crooks,
figures from a sauced-up sandman who, after wiping, runs for President.

14. EXILE IN IRONY

Settled several hours within the orbital aviary;
marshal swoops trundle in the distance,
powerful beyond the starship's auld diction;
the meters only confirm our dread,
in two weeks we plan on having no oxygen,
in four weeks we run out of food, but who cares;
yes, the tactical mind is piqued, but my
patience for pap smears and hemoglobin sticks has waned,
these practices had their day, but
now, the civic rays of the sunset blunt our mission;
send citizens, Romans, quarks and admen,
send a bunch of free junk, too, like chopsticks and matches,
—the whole kit-and-caboodle is starting to seem
like one angry Argonaut's idea of getting even,
and, inevitably, we will grow bored, and possibly vicious.

15. TRANSFERENCES

His dream was all literature but his prey ration was all puppies;
poppies produced the word, which sent him rolling
down the streets to the cemetery to the leopard in slacks;
after the hour had ended, he retied his slacks
and forgave the passing preachers their ignorance of his solidarity,
resembling as they did the driftwood on pale beaches;
now, there was a day to spend searching for the perfect aperitif,
which poisons to portend, which stanzas to brag of,
which of the famous wrists to stick a fork in, and which
of the educated young to usefully ignore;
by evenings he worked on translations of old French novels,
verbs plucked out for the girl with cinematic morals
inventing that teat for a squeeze though he rarely ever enjoyed it,
and arrogated himself to some dilemma conceived in a medieval youth,
—proud as the village illiterate who's just pawned the town key.

16. NITE FLIGHT

A short flight;
one alone into the forest
to glean the hut's location;
peasant fashion,
straw sandled and fists
in the torn pockets;
and the bubs
pure as mountaintops,
the ham too cold to touch
like poems;
finally, reaching the shoreline,
the first to see the Pacific,
beyond the dreams of Europe
and the video arcades,
setting a course for the family vision.

17. THE THIEF'S JOURNAL

We were walking quietly along the Czech border;
we were not concerning ourselves with women,
being hard-coded by the fracas to avoid them;
then nature, as in Genet, became maternal,
concealing, beyond anecdote, the murderers and princes,
though nothing lay in mist but stones, turds;
our first names were a precise deliverance, enough,
not not invented, but not hostile to identity,
the practices of *bands* criss-crossing the countryside
more than the comfort of using found names;
occasionally I would stutter, using her name
on the telephone, and when it was longer than two syllables,
I used another name, another woman's name, if I thought of one,
—this always happened, so that I gave up on names,
or simply used an acronym, until she became my confidante.

18. The thief's journal (2)

Stiltano's deadbeat hunger was merging into mine;
by the time I write these memoirs, he is dead,
struck by a cab outside a theater;
feeling free and resolved, I was a willful slave,
holding his lice and ill-luck, obscured
by his shadow darker than Africa's, and cursing;
perhaps this chronicle of vengeance
was rehearsed, a mere way to make a line-break
better than mundane, than the others, not less
rehearsed, yet never to be imitated;
losing the shape of the poem in the song
isn't nice, in fact it is a departure into arrogance
into a careless, bold attitude that spurns friends,
hiding in the ruses of melody the *interface*,
the contract and the gaze, the knowledge of your presence.

19. The thief's journal (3)

That was the number of the guy I phoned alone;
we became beads of sweat as Mount Fuji slipped
between rail cars like some royal excrement;
who would have troubled the conductor with this,
in sensitive situations it's best not to waver
between a dance and assurance, suggestive and wise;
the problem was unfolding by halves, and soon
would have subsumed the fog in windows
with its nickel-store sophisms, yes, weak penny-antics,
but for the automated witness of a digital Arcade;
Tokyo drenched our skin in teenage acid and televator boobs,
our time in the taxi oddly hyperbolic flight,
but like Byron to the Greeks, we took to their questions,
vital as we felt to the country's rash independence,
eventually coming upon its bold, empty circle of regret.

20. The reactionary

How is the creature to sleep, without a fiction to entertain;
they thought him a phalanx, all intellect and wit,
without substance, no one to see a movie with;
Eliotic, he brushed the dandruff from his collar and paid a visit,
needing no attention to his divagations, just
happy to be around, in Baltimore, and the last one speaking "English;"
because the soul oil of his pants, his stance,
his big romance with literature, his damnable self-sufficiency,
reeked of colons, periods, he wasn't dealt with,
but that's already been the subject of this poem's preceding paragraph;
now, two years closer to something unobtainable,
there is a new clarity in the nostrils, such that primitive intuitions
are precise, but this plays no role in the pantomime—
he torques, resists, revives, a parody of patriarch
and exercises his grand permissions upon the audience.

21. The stylist

Too much enjoyment in receiving sweet caresses;
on a gray day, it comes to an end, the choiring stops,
the hairless back is exposed and nose drips;
now, speech can move freely as the divorce is near total
and one wants, with diligence, to connect
without the compromise of economic betrayal in the effort;
a flatmate's radio plugs country tunes—none are concerned
for the groans of inattention from the Stylist
once gratifyingly regaled with dances of the intellect
and putrid encomiums and example scale progressions;
this is sounding bad, but the glow of futurity is upon him
now, Rimbaudian flair in the Humbertian flight,
in fact, this sobriety has its truth qualities
which one doesn't find in the gossip or party weeklies,
that is only discovered in the blacked out repose of the retina.

22. RESOLUTIONS

I don't choose to treat them like bad smells;
these poets may be smart, irreducible, practicing a lot
but you proceed to approach them like bad smells;
then there is the idea of *compromise,*
compromised from what, I'd have to ask—
as if avant-garde poetry should survive as a cottage industry;
it's become narrowed down to a blip,
the next step is to hit the power-off
and send the weakening signal to its horizon,
or perhaps send it to video, so you can recall it;
unless one wants to make an aesthetic of
its decay, fetishizing the moss that now surrounds it,
a private ecstasy among the tabaccoey odor of its infrastructure—
the voices within it, the old and dead,
becoming thus trapped within it, an old dead practice.

23. CARLYLE IN LONDON

I still won't know what to do;
the relevant comments, remarks,
filtered from a day of dropped clauses;
the NASDAQ responded
by tumbling from its high seat
into the flesh pit;
what was so incredible
was how everything seemed to matter again,
the flesh of the hand, the throb in the enraged neck,
the patterns songs took when extended;
and this got us thinking, after a while, talking,
perambulating in the garden like in the old days,
mumbling *objectif* and *subjectif* through pianola noses,
disarming with reference
the threats of those inhibiting you.

24. THE TYROS

Some writers will ignore you with the language;
"here is my flesh-eating heart," for
example, or blandly "paratactic" logorrhea;
these are the messages transmitted by page
and post, more than words: gestures
—and by gestures, E-zine, Techno, are being yoked;
to "fill out the meter," how grand, such
catastrophic spondees (the pun is on "sophist")
to write them and read them, such numb, flatulent whiffs
in which my narrative, sort of, proceeds;
but what surfaces from the noise except a new theory
of noise—"and no religions, too"—chalk poems on clipboards,
basking in the ragout of Black Bloc Seattle,
where the noise was nearly articulate, but was just noise
one expected from the State's petty scansion—so give me noise.

25. THE TYROS (2)

Triple sheets of paper do not make the key strike harder;
he pounds the ground with his fists, manages a moan,
but otherwise, emotions are strictly retarded;
Telex thinks this could be matter for prime-time, now
that the nation is relaxed, bohemians have jobs,
and a market's erupted from what was once a wealth of uncertainty;
—they discovered the torso in the trunk, it
spoke of something long forgotten, or they had struggled
to forget, racing for the thinly imaged goals
not bothering to remark those lost in historical bounty;
if a single chord could bark this confusion,
music would find the pitch of hearts otherwise inured to sound
but that's practically a page from the Futurist cookbook,
song and dance from a more serious, if rabid, cabal,
—those who could imagine nothing less than a social beauty.

26. OUTRO

A visit to the world's lobotomy;
in a thousand cantos, they think they've discovered it all,
and in acid washes, reduced it to megabytes;
funk me, selectric thrill,
pass my body to the language and shiver me timbers,
dalliance of a green-haired horse in Irish mythology;
the cousins kissed, under the ferns,
the camera clicked, and historical collusion fetishized its credit cards,
what computer to purchase next, what pumps
as the adjectives clasped;
after the relatives gasped, they opened a bottle of champagne
and their sturdy fortunes righted themselves for the progenetive walk
among the day-glo mushrooms and leper's votes
fraught with the violence of nouns,
so we must admire their singular determination.

Coda: "The Nineties tried your game"

"I have a problem with Mass Media"
—John Wieners

ৱ

1. YELLOW ATMOSPHERICS

The nanotechs blame God on botched magnetic resonance;
from there, we set off toward Croatoan,
indifferent to the intertonic *falsches* of mud;
what we got were indices rendering the old counts moot,
a cache of journalistic superlatives, bachelor-pad hagiographies,
cash-flows morphing into giga-*bluts*;
but no one could resist that image of a pure, pre-invested Orient, even
the Accomplished were at it, reading up on Espen Aarseth,
who cared not a nit for Susan Howe,
or for the traipsing across vascular lands burning Anabaptists;
for the Culture Wars were, in all quarters, over,
or so we thought—of the un-Bloomed, post-*huitarded*
world of informational Nascar—of the mentally clean-shaven
masses who listened intently (when surely the message was insane)
to the expensive disappearance… now, we are only alive.

2. An invocation: the tin god, etc.

We just aren't there yet;
(um, it's just a bunch of
people talking to themselves?);
Genoa can wait, so
can Pyongyang, this
suspension is most interesting;
spell-checked culture
with rhyme *with* reason,
and a salient, subjunctive peace
—until then, in arrears;
what man, god, or tin,
what flim-flam, humpty-dump, razzle-
dazzle articulates in chips,
spell-bound as the lad of Naxos
—but, for all that, the chirping of modems.

3. REGARDING WHERE THEY LIVED IN THOSE DANGEROUS TIMES

Given the goad, the virulent bail-out of the "Axis"—Exxons—"of Evil";
Pasha marshals the hackers, but mocks the hacked (in theory),
lassoes the snow of front lawns with margarita piss;
the Cave, however, exhibits solidarity—there is no truth in Nigeria
worth flying there for, no canon of anti-systemic hopes,
—thus, a follower, and dyslexic at that, he's wall-eyed, comatose;
the Rites of perfect meter won't send him slouching
toward Bethlehem, nor the boas of John Wheelwright, nor cruises with the editor
of *The Nation*, nor the muckraking of *The Voice*,
pull him onto the streets with his inky cleaver to proffer his minus;
virginal newness is the temper of his *debut-de-siècle*, Song
of American Drains—right here in Williamsburg no different, saddled with
British pallor, Balkan braggadocio, or Nipponese spikes,
making an ill-scanned Mermaid Day Parade of our *voyants* off to work
—shepherded to the L, vanguarded through the paperless office, shuffled off to hell.

4. Vague intimations of how they spend their time

You've acquired a few words with *-meme* in it;
such learning can speckle the wings
—the Bucky Ball inflates, from family to fraught habitus;
if society were an onion, you'd be crying,
they say—Ted, Mary, Lou, you'd be off the air in minutes,
crying—failed détente of the barely living;
arterial highways, a gelatinous, national couture
—children shrink-wrapped, staring from the shelves
awaiting their arrest, alienated, staring
into the sun—that is, until they learn their *memes*;
under the temple, down the backroom stairs, evasions
no longer hold, and they are volumes from Black Culture
—they are tourists at home, finding warmer
companions among the self-immolators of Prague,
—they've seen the original *Solaris* dozens of times, now the remake.

5. Some of the terrible things they dream

The skin is an organ, the face is an organ, the truth is an organ, the earth is an organ;
did the radio pronounce Barishnikov with the proper execution of diphthongs
and fricatives, and, if so, are we friends or ants, peers or doppelgangers;
the very rapid sex of fraternizing has created a bounty of sorts—the tapped words mish mash
and ungovern their latter tenses with names hardly functioning deictically,
hardly referencing their suasive dimensions;
search strings, cable trials, miscarries—vegetable consciousness is no ghost, rather
the work of British crop dusters who satisfy the mania
for finding Mandelbrot sets in what were once thought teaming, horny particles
produced by an Earth suffering chromosomic enema;
when War settled on the continent, still floundering in post-Surrealist *dériv*, knocking back
a few while trying to nudge the remote with a cauterized ass cheek,
the teleactive, the arduous, the omni-political, the photogenic (geeks)
propped Billy Beers on monitors and subjected them to streams of spit, to see
how they fell—and basing a decision on that, hacked the Brazilian Congress's dot gee oh vee.

6. FURTHER THOUGHTS ON THE STYLIST

Not assured of the hedonist's rapture, or of the safety of guiding ropes;
he has a normal name otherwise, nothing to suggest television,
drinks too much perhaps, is over-studied for literary conflagration;
the list, after that, grew blurry, once including: "syncresis," "allotropes,"
"Marxism" (also, "Leninism," "Stalinism") and "individualist"
for contrast, also "humanism," "realism" (vs. "social realism"), madly "Darwinist";
in Vancouver, these are just the names of punk bands, all
frissons to rumbles, prismatic (where Stateside they would be "dualists")
paragrammatic, enabling the Revolution by frobbing syntactical dials
—forgetting, before the Moderns, we claimed Bliss Carman for "ourselves";
Williams would have loved him, just as likely Pound, Zukofsky, and Marianne
Moore, his neighbor, but for us he's Ashbery-meets-Gibson (William,
not Mel), Philip K. Dick channeling Spicerian Lenny Bruce through old coffee radio
of insomniac Chomskyite nites—perfectionist, though perhaps no Gautier
(Theophile) in form—a word without embellishment, sans Vorpal Sword, only contacts.

7. The television begins to act upon their nostrils

What burst upon his revelry but an allergenic spoor, a sneeze;
Pound's flopping of oars, this one marked "Anhedonist,"
forcing him across the floor, to unlock the door, then re-lock;
we can funkify the seediness of this des Esseintes moment with digits
insatiable, or with crises that approach with the grace
of guttural, 32-bit Nazis, or with jodi.org's antique, "pro-situ" strains;
his Polish friends didn't visit anymore (if they ever did), not since
Jeffrey Deitch moved in, then out (after 9/11), and then in
came the fashions—ever-more-clawed-at hairstyles, "hacked apart
by a brainless cretin" (Eno), for the twenty-something post-collegiates, mainly white;
"there's always Butoh to aspire to," Pasha pondered, or (dialectically)
the converse, Min Tanaka's gravity—"I didn't leap, I fell"—on the roof
of P.S. 1, summer 1999, last year anyone cared about
the turn of the millennium, or U2, or "sampling," or Language Poetry, or Michel
Foucault—imagining for the moment that absence commands authority.

8. The mobilization prospers—with a few hitches

HVA and Pasha proceeded to plan their "War Number;"
this incurred much skepticism from their friends in Toronto
and New York where, respectively, they lived;
the question was collecting work invested in the theme
of war, which neither of them had seen, or merely
on TV—even as they culled their title from the second issue of *Blast*;
submissions were varied—word salads, holy screeds,
some with perspective, some less diaristic
than others—some of it even well-researched—most taking
four pages to get to the subject (which it choked);
Pasha, as editor, was publicly generous, as was
HVA, though in private they were criminally incensed
by what they'd fueled—baroque variations on the office of "poet"
in Oceania, in cults of the Welsh, in the Cabaret Voltaire,
—dressed to the hilt for such selves, but not, presumably, right here.

9. AFTER SURPRISING ELECTIONS

Survival of the glibbest;
avant-garde terrorists
refusing to be so named;
my potluck dreams adorn
a trailer park, yes
a post-Arcadian blankness;
waiting for the ripped
facade, the squeal of *saving face*
in feinting quatrains
to come ribboning down;
satellites of youth deference
abound, we feel so
bold among the cancer lovers,
but I'm finally learning to write
again, amid the bungalows and sands.

10. We leave them mid-circle—with no assurances

The "Nineties" tried your game, and hiccoughed a Babel, of course;
portending a plunderphonic adrenalin rush at the *fin-de-siècle*,
a sort of fight-or-flight mentality, a decadent mulch, or bombed steel twist;
that's how it feels, flounder-eyed at the bottom
of a century—thinking on the one hand there's Moxley, and on the other
that Canadian who levels Perec against the bits;
nothing but celluloid seems very old, these days, the first
of the trope-recycling "new" arts in cahoots with Benjamin's Golden Age,
—rather than calcium in bones, we have the half-life of Jean Vigo,
which, if this seems confusing, is, really, quite OK;
books will continue to be made, and Johnson (Lionel) will still fall from the stool,
I'll bribe you with these allusions, Auden will continue to be chthonic in September
1932, and we'll still complain that Barbara Guest was (literally) a parenthesis
in David Lehman's *The Last Avant-Garde*, and we'll be carpet-bombed with poems,
until the big novel hits
                              —in which case there will still be Tom Phillips' *A Humument*.

from The Screens

"With punk, a brand-new axis opened up: *professionally cut* ⇔ *hacked about by a brainless cretin*. As often happens, this appeared (and was intended) to be an anti-style style, and was shocking because we had never previously considered the possibility that the concept 'style' and the concept 'hacked about by a brainless cretin' could overlap one another. But, as usual, the effect was not to overthrow and eliminate the idea of style but to give it new places in which to extend itself. [...] What characterizes fundamentalism is a set of extremely narrow axes that allow almost no movement, no experimentation."
—Brian Eno, "Axis thinking"

Axis Thinking

ॐ

Ambient ⇔ "Idiot energy." "Plain speech" ⇔ Baroque. Eliot's idea of "good" (Goethe) ⇔ Eliot's idea of "evil" (Baudelaire). The poetry of bulk ⇔ Arid extra dry. Boy those Asians are smart ⇔ Boy those Asians are dumb. The Who ⇔ The Beatles. Helen Keller/Arakawa ⇔ Anthony Hecht/Yasusada. The standard ⇔ The non-standard. Cult of speed (Bruce Andrews) ⇔ Cult of slowness (Mei-mei Bersenbrugge). Utopia (punk) ⇔ Fatalism (grunge). Fashion ⇔ Ethics. Extreme ⇔ Center. Pragmatism (American) ⇔ Catholicism (French). Gertrude Stein ⇔ Ezra Pound. Steve McCaffery ⇔ Ezra Pound. John Cage ⇔ Ezra Pound. John Cage ⇔ Ian Hamilton Finlay. Tall and skinny (variable foot) ⇔ Short and fat (iambic pentameter). Cadence (vowels) ⇔ Percussion (consonants). A cabal of malcontents ⇔ A stable of professionals. Horizontal (social) ⇔ Vertical (private). Kevin Davies ⇔ Ange Mlinko. Soliloquy ⇔ Dialogue. A poetics of information ⇔ A poetics of achievement. The large canvas (*I Don't Have Any Paper So Shut Up, or Social Romanticism*). ⇔ The small canvas (*The Collected Poems of Robert Creeley*). Monotheism ⇔ Polytheism. Collage ⇔ Pleine air. Stone ⇔ Paper. Paper ⇔ Screen. Screen ⇔ Garden. Literary tradition (Jennifer Moxley) ⇔ Literary lineage (Robert Fitterman). Improvisation/Originality (Tim Davis) ⇔ Mastery/imitation (Miles Champion). Homage ⇔ Insult. West Coast (slow, meditative, attractive coloration, subtle changes in the weather) ⇔ East Coast (fast, schizophrenic, threatening coloration, profound changes in the weather). Rockstar (Jim Morrison) ⇔ Wallflower (Joseph Cornell). Exhibitionist ⇔ Virtuoso. Reading ⇔ Parsing. Beauty ⇔ Experience. A human-scale Thomas Pynchon ⇔ A cosmic-scale Robbe-Grillet. Australia ⇔ Canada. Form ⇔ Flux. Critics who can write poetry ⇔ Critics who can't write poetry. Edmund Berrigan ⇔ Anselm Berrigan. Memory through madeleines (Marcel Proust) ⇔ Experience through chickens (William Carlos Williams). Debut volume (forgotten) ⇔ Posthumous volume (returned). The language of birds ⇔ The language of priests. Juvenile ⇔ Assimilated. Encyclopedic/paratactic ⇔ Homeric/narrative. Encyclopedic/Homeric ⇔ Positivistic/personal. Pretending you don't have something you have ⇔ Pretending you have something you don't have. Charles Olson ⇔ Lyn Hejinian. Music for thinking ⇔ Music for fucking. Anthemic (Bruce Springsteen/Queen) ⇔ Operatic (David Bowie/Queen). First generation New York School

⇔ The other generations of the New York School. Pious avant-gardism (classroom) ⇔ Raucous avant-gardism (carnival). William Poundstone ⇔ John Cayley. Pantheism ⇔ Idealism. Poems made of foam ⇔ Poems made of stone. Sentence ⇔ Fragment. "I don't know how humanity stands it with a painted paradise at the end of it, without a painted paradise at the end of it" ⇔ "Poetry is like a swoon but with this difference: it brings you to your senses." Volcanic idiom ⇔ Therapeutic idiom. Vancouver ⇔ Toronto.

Um, Uh

❧

Um, they're, um, uh, yeah everybody, uh, staring at you? Uh, you're, um, uh, the only black person here? Uh, I don't, uh, um, like those *shows*. Um, you're, uh, a little, er, tipsy? Uh, your, uh, wall-eye is, yeah, acting up. You, uh, have a little issue with, er, um, your shorts. You, er, could have used, ah, a little more, uh, deodorant. Uh, you, er, are making a lot of references to, uh, hmm, your mother? Um, I think, er, there's a little, uh, activity on your cheek there? Um, are those poppy seeds, er, seem caught in, er, your teeth. Er, I think, uh, you should put your hand back, yeah. Your lunch, um, seems to be, er, coming back? Those, um, trousers are, uh, a bit *high tide*. Um, are you, er, a bit, uh, shy with men? Um, I think you're, er, supposed to leave a, yeah, leave a tip. Um, I think, er, you, um, have a little hang-up with T.S. Eliot? Uh, how can I say this, er, you have a little, uh, thingy, er, uh, yeah, on your thingy, uh huh. Uh, that, er, pimple... yeah. Er, uh, I think that, um, poem was written, er, in, uh, 1939? Um, I think that, er, screensaver is, uh, a little, yeah, offensive, um, to, you know, um, short people? Um, I think you could, er, maybe, uh, buy me a drink now? You should probably, er, uh, cross your legs? I think , um, you could, er, talk a little, uh, yeah, quieter. Um, that, er, you just sort of, uh, spit on me? Aren't you, um, a little short, uh, to be a storm trooper? Um, I think, er, you should, uh, cover up that, yeah, scar? Um, isn't that, er, uh, like, enough cigarettes for a night? Um, er, didn't, uh, Vito Acconci do that already? Um, aren't there, er, places you could, yeah, put that? Um, er, your, uh, accent, er, yeah, nobody can under-stand you. Um, is that, er, toothpaste on your, uh, collar, um? Uh, I think that's, er, uh, your brother, yeah, stopping traffic over there. *I could be wrong.* Um, isn't that, er, a little, uh, obviously pretentious. Er, uh, wasn't, er, Keats born, uh, a century *before* Swinburne? Er, I, uh, think you've been, uh, yeah, let other people talk a bit, huh? Er, uh, I don't think, er, you should be clipping your toenails just this second, no. You, uh, have a little, uh, whip cream? Uh, isn't your vocal style, er, a bit, er, uh, circa 1978 Patti Smith? Um, isn't , uh, playing with the fonts, er, a bit, uh, hm, yeah, old? Um, I think there's, uh, a bit too much, er, *(coughs)* garlic in this *(coughs)*. Um, I think your, er, yeah, is, uh, hanging a little low. Uh, I think, um, you're, uh, yeah, aren't you slurring? Um, isn't that, er, a, um, long-winded explanation? Um, don't you owe me, eh, fifty dollars? Um, I think, er, you, uh, yeah, probably a little gas. Um, aren't you just, er, kind of, uh, gossiping? Isn't that, like, uh, er, anti-Semitic? You seem to be, uh, a little bit, er, shiny today, yeah. You have your, uh, elbows on the, er, yeah, right. Um, don't you think, er, you should, uh, stop, yeah, that's *dancing?* Um, why do you, er, keep shaking your leg, uh? Er, I think there's a bit, er, much crotch action there? Um, there, are, uh, women in this room, er, maybe your jokes are a bit, er, um, misogynistic. Uh, are you, uh, something of a, uh, er, mouth breather? I think you should try, uh, a little bit of this, er, lip balm, huh? Uh, that isn't, er, the, um, way to *make friends.* This is, um, a, er, a funeral? Your, um, flies unzipped? Um, uh, you seem to be, er, repeating, er, yeah, yourself. Isn't that, uh, joke a bit, uh, Regis Philbin? Er, isn't that, um, a bit of your, um, yeah, sticking out? Um, you, you're, uh, um, foaming? Um, you, er, should probably be, uh, a little more, uh, subtle about gay people? Um, uh, I think you, uh, should answer your cellular? Er, your face is, uh, em, just beat red? Um, you are, er, uh, yeah I think, *chronically depressed?*

Social Cripples

ॐ

A poet once passed on a little witticism to me that has stuck in my mind and, indeed, been quite useful in reflection on the occasionally troublesome way that people interact in the writing community: "All poets are social cripples." It's certainly something I've suspected. As Christian Bök once said to me, he is willing to put up with the most "rebarbative" of people provided they are good artists. I could have suggested that most good artists are rebarbative, that they almost always seem primed for some attack, some threat to their ontological status as infinitely ingenious creative and thinking beings. Where could one go with such an "insight," if one is willing to grant this witticism anything suggesting philosophical import? I tend to think of it along the lines of something Richard Rorty has written about language (deriving, he claims, from the writings of linguist Donald Davidson), that the function of language is to make people more "predictable" to others. Try it: walk into a room of people and not say anything for a half hour, and relish the tension in the air. It's a good, basic, portable truth which hardly suffices as a grand theory of language, but which, nonetheless, brings into focus a large portion of what one might consider the "content" of poetry. If all language, even the most basic such as that used when purchasing oranges (the classic example always seems to be the language used in commerce) is merely some version of foreign policy, then certainly all language is charged with implications that extend beyond one's involuntary sublimation of its import. Which is to say, there are some elements of foreign policy that we are all quite comfortable with; most of us can safely walk into a store and purchase "oranges" without much psychological trauma. Likewise, not many interesting poems are going to be created based on the specific qualities of this interaction. Certainly one could deterritorialize the transaction to suggest the interrelation of it with the Spectacle or global economy (an interesting poem, perhaps a funny one like that by Steve McCaffery that is a baroque over-description of a conventional "hello"). Likewise, one could sentimentalize it, tie buying "oranges" into a nostalgic reminiscence of buying "oranges" in Czechoslovakia in 1977 (a bad poem). The point being: poets spend so much time troubling the issues of foreign relations, and interesting, engaged poets tend to do this troubling along the entire range of relations from introduction to the seductive embrace, terrorizing manufactured consent, chipping away fervent-

ly at the canon, not to mention purchasing "oranges," that it is no won-
der they end up social cripples—all language has been so incredibly
deterritorialized, which is to say, made "uncanny," that the engines are
most likely not able to be turned off when talking over some basic issue
like baseball scores or haircuts. I notice that I am writing my worst
poems when I feel most comfortable in the "community," and that, when
I am perceived as somewhat friendly, my poems are rather bland
attempts at continuing good relations. This is merely one approach one
could take to this issue.

Italics

ॐ

Sort of: being there, or being *awake*. | These emissions: counter-examples of *honesty*. | Trying: being in the *type*. | A calculated instance (among distrust): lost in *Europe*. | We thought it was Dutch: it was *Flemish*. | As in: where to go *next*. | Running out of drink, then: where is the *fountain*. | Trying: to angle the *light*. | Grossly spiritual, she takes a number: she is *waiting*. | Productive backslide: thinking back to *terms*. | I am here: you are *there*. | How many times have you been there: and I've *choked*. | A sliver of counter-honesty: spicy *discussion*. | Nonetheless, remembering: *remembering*. | The crowd was fucked: *fucked*. | Bouncing a ball: waiting for the next *line*. | Moment by moment, the web was built: *falters*. | Later: taking a *test*. | That writer who wrote of love and fame: that writer who *died*. | Production ceased: of *course*. | Making noises with the pen: scratch, *tap*. | And when she turns to me: forgetting *amnesty*. | The life gets better, but the writing: *worse*. | Dialing up: tuning (getting) *out*. | Indecision is insufferable: then, the *rain*. | When the masculine forecloses: athletic *poem*. | A drop: then, *sound*. | Trying: negotiating a *wave*. | Thinking it was Cage, knowing finally: *Eno*. | Pacing back and forth, smoking, fidgeting: *behavior*. | Cars on the highway: moving forth into *adventure*. | When it bleeds: *satire*. | Scanning the crowd for the familiar: *faces*. | Two words together that make a dull story: *theory*. | Crying: public *address*. | Anticipating: public *demonstrations*. | When the polls close: catharsis of the new *naive*. | On the streets, garbage, dust: *sediment*. | I think: I have *invented*. | Blowing the nose into an ashtray: improbable *dis - sent*. | The pathology of getting it wrong: *dada*. | Trying to circulate among nuance: flexing the *Jamesian*. | And when the table cleared, and the conversation ceased: my *family*. | Birds warble: *morning*. | Cheap jokes and laughing gas: *community*. | The image profoundly dithers: the site is *ugly*. | When the chips are finally counted: *pragmatism*. | No longer: puppet of *stars*. | No longer: victim of the *contiguous*. | No longer: angling to be a stable *critic*. | After a failure of short-term memory: renew the *streets*. | Every temp its turn: every type its *torque*. | Drinking the wine: marrying the *incredible*. | Pausing before words, inhaling: anticipating *commotion*. | Taking the wrench to technology: curbing the *linear*. | Bathing, paring, shaving: *detoxifying*. | Exploring the real estate of the block: inveigling the *dogs*. | Loving by brush of the cheek: evading the *secular*. | Futzing with the stocks, rolling with the hunches: the quizzical *mine.* | Pissing: *watching.* | Making controversy on the blog: stemming literary *conversion.* | The laughs get better, the writing: *worse.* | Running away to Canada, running away to Patagonia: *syllables.* | Chuckling in Cathedrals: instantiating *echoes.* | With an eye on the ball: with a hand on the *clutch.* | Knee shakes, rhythmically: *manic.* | Korean soup-eater sips loudly: her comforting *music.* | Glass backboard after youth smashing basketball against flaccid metal one: *hubris.* | Argument settled, friendship adhered: check *paid.* | We know the news when we refuse the headlines: disciplined *scanning.* | In the dope: after the *anxiety.* | Naughty movie business: suburban *voyeurism.* | No longer: fingering the *watch-chain.* | No longer: sinking behind *make-up.* | I mean: it must *be.* | Wanting the throat to be Chinese: getting *Sicilian.* | New airport screening rules: new sentience in the *database.* | Revisiting photographs: deep-freezing the *enigmas.*

Reading Pound

ৡ

All the best traits of English prosody died with you, my friend. *Compleynt,* *compleynt,* I hear it every day: the voices are singular, but advertised as reproductions. Lifeless air becomes sinewed; the vagaries of the potlatch arraign the man, the woman, in cobwebs of involuntary capital—the clear air, dark, dark, the dead concepts, never the soldering but homely swarms of poor confidence, over-elaborated arguments, good scholarship and the bad, all "going down with the ship." So then go down to the ship, set heel to sneakers, froth on the motley sneers, and stammer mash and swill on that scholarship: when the parse is good, the pass is pointworthy. But a lady blasts me; she speaks of "reason," some wild effect that is dumb if too often, some monotheism in the face of plurality—and of that, there are several varieties. Cooking up some forgotten predecessor out of the drafts of time, from time, who even dead yet hath our minds entire—finding some lost continent in the vortex, reaching land, the sea streaked *rouge rouge rouge* (Chopin). Outdated books of anthropology, rites that never were but in Gessel's imagination, hearing the roots speak together, Pollocks on Schneider patents, orders from Paris and.... all have been tried. Anyone can pun to excess, it is hard to run past the mark, it is easy to stand firm in the middle, somewhere between a Dean Democrat and a Compassionate Conservative—muckraker alliteration will be the death of us. When you are obvious, my friend, you are most proactive; your sneakers float above theory, these exchanges bearing abundance, and the prisons become empty. "Don't waste your time... because the gosh-darn girl is mine..." I heard over the waters, and "The country is over-brained," said the Hungarian nobleman—because the Austrians need a Buddha, they spell words with a drum beat, and the Koreans need a buddy, they spell words with a phonetic script that was invented in the thirteenth century. It doesn't get good until the action starts, and you realize the extra square footage of your apartment with feng shui—thus, we have another aspect, which we will call the financial aspect, giving us the power to buy (wages, dividends), but also the comfort to write in the ease of Bahama temperatures. "A poet is like a small business," said Berrigan; and again, "Anyone can run to excess... it is hard to stand firm in the middle." My friend: there was a goddess of the fair knees, and she split a bottle of wine with me while we listened to Christian Bök do the *Ursonate* in ten minutes flat, the only two people in the world who shared this experience among the dead concepts, full of knowing that the beefy man knew less than us. But my meanings are opaque: I am reading through the parts of Ezra Pound's *Cantos* included in his *Selected Poems*, and trying to attach my own meanings to the lines, forming like a diafan from light on shade the meters that mattered to me most when in high school—honor to Brian Kim Stefans, the surveyor. I'm late for brunch; in the 40th year of King Quang died Kung aged 73. Did we fall because of our taste in music? "Hey! none of that mathematical music here," they shouted, expecting tubas and violins and not mouse pads and laptops, samples and sine waves; yet, ere the session died of scold and discontent, an ambience was created for the conversation, and music straddled speech with speech not even trying—my breath, *per - sonae*, became the light, *virtú*. I'd want to say these words find their way to the screen with no help from me; I'd want the green light to gleam in this sheen, tile upon tile, pale in the wine-red algae... but no. Even the high-falutin' bidness of Denis Roche cannot keep the accidents out of this poem; moving to the right border, moving to the other side, moving back, my questions are inevitable, and she hears me somehow in Los Angeles: Mt. Taishan to my sunset. A lizard upholds me... Reptilian Neolettrist Graphics; but who is there left for me to shore a joke with? What ant's a centaur in this drag-queen world?

We Make

২

We make fecal jokes. We make jokes out of time. We make noises that humiliate us in front of our neighbors. We make trees stand together to form paper. We make obvious jokes. We make clouds stand still for the photograph. We make babies out of food. We make self-propagating programs that we call "worms." We make coffee. We make self-governing groups of people that we call "teams." We make impressions on our skin, permanent or semi-permanent. We make tents. We make cigarettes. We make cheese. We make earrings out of shells. We make plastic body parts out of our ability to melt things. We make unlikely drinks. We make fantastic jokes. We make movable parts that are in motion to the metrics of the seas. We make sunglasses to stare at the sun. We make moustaches. We make wallets out of skin. We make shoes out of skin. We make coats out of skin, being bashful about our own skin, and insecure in general. We make virtues out of our vulnerabilities. We make concepts. We make plans. We make bags, we fill them with stolen items. We make movies that we call "popular" or "classics," occasionally "popular classics" We make burrows like hedgehogs and name them "A," "F" and "6." We make hotels and never sleep in them. We make "printers" and never write on them. We make televisions and never appear on them, nor do we televise anything. We make cigarettes (did I mention that already?). We make cars but can't drive them to Germany. We make planes but most of us don't fly them. We make bookshelves and write books, also. We make kimchi, not quite as quickly as we make hot dogs, but we do. We make unique phrases out of old, already used ones. We make jellies, ones you can eat and ones that burn. We make soap. We make dirt, but not on purpose. We make plans, and as we ruin them, we make "progress." We make inscrutable jokes. We make constitutions out of what were once just communal fixations. We make myths out of the most ordinary individuals. We make certainties out of an incubating cloud of doubts. We make starlets out of the most ordinary, female material. We make "plays." We make lists. We make steam out of tormenting water with heat. We make sauces out of corrupting the aforementioned water. We make industries out of water, also. We make flesh, even when we're sleeping. We make "arrangements," sometimes in the home, sometimes in the park. We make parks out of trees that could have better been used for paper. We make odors (this is also usually involuntary). We make jokes about them. We make religions out of fear, but also the ability to make things too complex. We make noises out of air, even when it has its own noise. We make sentences. We make divorces. We make slam. We make hard. We make gerunds, and sometimes they make gerunds but sometimes they can't make proper "gerunds." We make hearsay out of information. We make "journeys" out of "trips." We make "jokes" as byproducts of undiagnosed misanthropy. We make "essays" out of classroom notes. We make memories, or so I have heard. We make more flesh just listening to this, and just typing. We make music out of noise. We make "novels" out of our communal self-regard, and despite their name, they are often not "novel" at all. We make "leaders" out of self-proclaimed "leaders." We make "healers" out of those with a talent for the scalpel (they are also sadists). We make cuts in the salami (but not with scalpels). We make family events and serve the salami. We make riddles out of platitudes. We make crossword puzzles out of history's ungoverned proliferation, when it falls into language. We make guitars out of trees. We make rhythms out of watches (and hitting guitars). We make thoughts out of insomnia. We make "Trojan horses" out of comfortable elements in the landscape. We make light out of sulfur, usually in the process of desiring heat. We make blankets out of cotton, out of sheep, or just anything that lives, and has leaves, or skins. We make noises that silence the audience. We make shovels, we make art. We make jokes to punctuate the bad news. We make good news out of bad news in an effort to avoid new orthodoxies. We make high ceilings in central post offices in an effort to supplant old religions. We make mirrors that are hundreds of floors high. We make "skylines." We make "waistlines" (again, in our sleep). We make "skylines," thus, yes, but again, most of us don't make them. We make cities at the intersections of rivers. We make lists of money, often more elegantly than lines of poetry. We make saliva when we talk, somehow anticipating food. We make food out of talk. We make three spellings out of words that sound the same, "through," "threw" and "thru" for instance. We make insecure people out of wisely impassive people. We make "writers" out of people with no ability to do anything else. We make "havoc" out of places of pristine, sublime and evocative stasis. We make perverts out of huggable, avuncular people. We make "crimes" out of situations that are unremarkable. We make colas out of chemicals (and commercials). We make women out of men, and men out of misprisions of women. We make grammars that are "correct" to deem other grammars "incorrect." We make mores, and if you don't stick by them, in order to save you some humiliation, we make "originality," and in special instances, we adopt the category "sui generis," in order to put you in there and leave it all fashionably, disarmingly inscrutable. We make magazines that arrive with the frequency of waves. We make quiet out of unread magazines. We make "stories" out of half-heard "tales." We make laws out of fear. We make number sequences, like the Fibonacci, out of—oh, I don't know. We make animals out of water, some of which look like us. We make platelets in our marrows. We make synapses in our wombs. We make fetal (or fecal) jokes out of this prehistoric memory. We make "territories" out of triangulations marked by spots of urine. We make remarks of unintended kindness out of undernourished witticisms. We make art out of bankruptcy. We make gurus out of the unhealthy propagators of "charisma." We make politics out of unsorted data. We make weather reports that are never true. We make sheets of paper. We make numbers. We make cold people out of dead people. We make cold people out of our own never visited relatives. We make prophecies, when really we should be making observations. We make anticipations of biological finality when we fail to make use of flesh, air, and time. We make music that could soothe the soul, but often softens the wallet. We make music that humiliates us before our neighbors. We make texts that are easy to memorize, and texts that are difficult to recommend to parents. We make poems that sound like other poems. We make stanzas, we make glue, we make treachery out of trust, we make codas out of what were once highly anticipated, fresh beginnings.

Idea for Poem

꒐

You must feel absolutely safe before starting. *(idea for poem)* Afterwards, you can collect the sheets. *(idea for poem)* Tinny or bassy music of the neighbors blasting through the walls. *(idea for poem)* Walking to the white signs with Julie; green haze; chasing chimeras. *(idea for poem)* Solemn conversations; blue aging faces; tickets for Bangor, Maine. *(idea for poem)* Hardly noticing his battered head, thinking he's drunk. *(idea for poem)* Manipulate this series. *(idea for poem)* A closed set of references. *(idea for poem)* Language poetry said it brought you deeper into the writing. *(idea for poem)* 6 a.m. skies over Bard college; mist; chapel in distance; inappropriate gestures; touching. *(idea for poem)* All your bad poems, in Keds, coming to haunt you. *(idea for poem)* Knock knock jokes, all of them, she said. *(idea for poem)* Mere rhythm—dissent! *(idea for poem)* Cutting the paper in half. *(idea for poem)* There is the object of your admiration. *(idea for poem)* As if: seeing is admiration. *(idea for poem)* The majestic heights of the Cavalier poets; athletic figures in the dearth of amorous veneration. *(idea for poem)* Perfume on a stick. *(idea for poem)* All the misspellings in a perfect-bound book. *(idea for poem)* Last as long as the others—try to survive. *(idea for poem)* Eno soundtrack over atrocities of war. *(idea for poem)* The disjunct adjunct: ESL engendering [engineering] a new breed. *(idea for poem)* Julie still walking toward the signs; 6 a.m. skies over Bard college; same mist; same chapel; same glue. *(idea for poem)* We tell the stories that avert humiliation. *(idea for poem)* 100+ days of Bush and still breathing. *(idea for poem)* Still smoking. *(idea for poem)* We'll remember him. *(idea for poem)* The 1995 poetry conference in New York where you met everyone important to you. *(idea for poem)* 6 years later, you are no longer speaking to any of them. *(idea for poem)* They were incomplete, those poems, mere scratches against the slate (dada), compared to now, in which they are marble blocks on the landscape (neo-dada). *(idea for poem)* So: baby yourself with a fine carpet, warm socks, coffee, cigarettes, and try to write. *(idea for poem)* Humor should not be docile; reference should not be oblique. *(idea for poem)* Dehydration produces weird moiré patterns on the retina, industrial drones in the ears. *(idea for poem)* The interesting "dog among dogs" disposition: W. C. W.'s philosophy of floundering. *(idea for poem)* Or: Bill Luoma's "lazy philosophy." *(idea for poem)* Other sorts of tricks to avoid political disaffection—in a time without clocks! *(idea for poem)* She said, We need more narrative immersion, and less academic mewling. *(idea for poem)* Wandering—an old urbanism—renting—what we are left with now. *(idea for poem)* Computer not sure where to put the hyphen. *(idea for poem)* The radio is silent; so are we. *(idea for poem)* Julie's head is on her arm; her fingers brush the surface of the sea. *(idea for poem)* A renewed faith in the powers of chance: why I think small press circulation is not as interesting as the web. *(idea for poem)* This page is meeting our goals. *(idea for poem)* One of these lines will survive—the statistics suggest it. *(idea for poem)* Titles for prog-rock albums: medieval looking syllables, Arthurian affect, animals. *(idea for poem)* Trying to avoid self-consciousness, as in this poem. *(idea for poem)* Pale imitations of Darren-Wershler Henry andor rubber socks for every sort of missile. *(idea for poem)* Having lost the thread of thought which started a half-hour ago with Julie at Bard. *(idea for poem)* Trip to Toronto in July suggesting to me: travel means nothing. *(idea for poem)* I never had any problems with EMI. *(idea for poem)* User-defined paper sizes. *(idea for poem)*

Tulubun

৯

Hu us nurvuus mun wuth nurvuus uy's, guung ubuut nurvuus busunuss. Uf Tulubun cutch hum ut hus sucrutuve wurk thuy wull cunsudur hum un un'my uf Uslum ✚ buut hum up un struut bufure luckung hum uwuy. "Ut us cruzy, knuw U, uxpusung mysulf ▶ dungur luke thus," hu suys. "Uvun nuw, thunk U um U undur survuulluncu. Whut uf um U urrusted? huve U chuldrun suppurt tu." But thus us durung lufe hu hus chusun fur humsulf—lufe uf tuluvusuun rupuurmun. "Yus," hu suys. "Thunk U um U sumuune bruvu." Un must nutuuns, tuluvusuun muy bu wustu uf tume ✚ curruptung unfluuncu. But un Ufghunustun ut us supmly ullugul. Nu uwnung. Nu wutchung. Nu rupuurung. Undur rulung Tulubun's sturn unturprututuun uf Uslum, humun furm us nut ▶ bu dupucted un muvung ur stull pucturus. Thus ductum us unfurced by ruluguuus pulucumun frum Munustry fur Prumutuun uf Vurtuu ✚ Pruvuntuun uf Vucu. Thuy rude uruund un puckup trucks wuth scuwls un thuur fucus ✚ uutumutuc wuupuns ut thuur sudus. But muny Ufghuns huve rufused ▶ luve wuthuut thuur tuluvusuun pruvulugus. Thuy wunt ▶ suu wurld's vuduu muntuge—turred luvurs, fumuly crusus, upuc buttlus, rucruuted dususturs, rumuntuc cumudy. Dum gluw uf tuluvusuun scruun furtuvuly lughts thuusunds uf ruums un uuch uf Ufghunustun's mujur cutuus. Huw muny puuplu wutch furbuddun ul'c-truc bux? Ut us duffucult suy tu. Hure un Kunduhur, just us un cutuus uf Kubul ✚ Hurut, quustuun luuds ▶ wude spun uf guussus, frum 15 purcunt ▶ 80 purcunt. Tuluvusuun rupuurmun—whu pruvuded psu-udunym Juhun Mur fur sufuty's suke—ussumus truth ▶ bu tuwurd hughur ustumutu. But thun hus judgmunt us dusturted by cumpuny hu kuups, turbuned cuuch pututuus uf thus truubled cuuntry, whuch hus undured 22 cunsucutuve yuurs uf wur. "Sume uf Tulubun wutch tulu-vusuun tuu, uv'n fuw cummundurs," sued Mr. Mur, spuukung un Unglush. "Thuur uy's upun vury wudu, ✚ thuy rumumbur uv'rythung. Thuy cun tull yuu uxuctly whure thuy wure whun thuy wure wutchung whut muvuu." Unduud, ut us muvuus—bruught uluve un smull vuduu duscs—thut ure huurt uf thus nutuun's clundustune unturtuunmunt undustry. Tulubun cuntrul ubuut 90 purcunt uf Ufghunustun's turrutu-ry ✚ thuy rufuse ▶ ulluw tuluvusuun stutuun ▶ bruudcust un uny uf ut. Furuugn chunnuls cun bu pucked wuth rught huukup but unly smull numbur uf must dufuunt puuplu rusk tulltule uutduur plucumunt uf uv'n smull sutullute dush. Su muvuus must suffucu, duscs kupt un cuncu-ulmunt, us ure TV's ✚ vuduu CD pluyurs thumsulvus. Uf uffundurs ure cuught thuy usuully rucuuve une ▶ thruu munths un prusun, uccur-dung ▶ puuplu hure un Kunduhur. Thuur uquupmunt us dustruyed. "But uf thuy fund yuu wuth sux muvuu, thut's much wursu, thruu yuurs un juul," Mr. Mur sued duurly. "Thus us vury bed bucuuse must Umurucun fulms huve sux. Yuu ure buttur uff wutchung kung fu muvu-us ur Rumbu ur muvuus frum Unduu, whuch ure vury pupulur." Tuluvusuun rupuurmun us ulsu muvuu smugglur. Hu puruuducully mukus fuvu-huur druve ▶ Quuttu, un Pukustun, ▶ buy nuw unus. Tulubun suurch fur cuntrubund ut thuur chuckpusts, whure thuy thun duspluy shrudded rumnunts uf whut thuy huve duscuvured. Mr. Mur hudus hus cupuus uf buutlugged muvuu duscs un hulluwud-uut ruduu. "Uctuully, smugglung us uusy," hu sued. "Muny druvurs huve huddun cumpurtmunts un thuur curs. Muvuus ure bug busunuss. Yuu cun sull thum fur 200 rupuus," ubuut $3. Mr. Mur hus smull shup—nuthung mure thun stull, ruully—un une uf muny buzuurs un dusty Kunduhur, cuty uf ubuut 500,000 un udgu uf Rugustun Dusurt. Thure ure muny ul'ctrunucs sturus un uruu—✚ nune ure much ▶ luuk ut. Gutted cur sturuus ure puled une utup uthur. Fruyed wurus dunglu frum cuulung. Brukun untunnus, urphuned by dued sugnuls, luu ucruss wuudun tublus. Pupulur musuc us ulsu bunned un Ufghunustun, but rucurdungs uf unuccumpunued chuntung by Tulubun fuuthful ure uvuulublu un uuduu cussuttus. Thus muuns thut used sturuus cun bu duspluyed upun-ly, thuur uld plustuc fucus sturung uut thruugh nuw plustuc cuvurung. Smull, tumuwurn, duscruut TV's sull un bluck murkut fur ubuut $50. "Thu Tulubun uxpuct yuu ▶ wurk ✚ pruy ✚ du nuthung ulsu un butwuun," tuluvusuun rupuurmun gruusud, luukung uut ut struut us busy wuth dunkuy curts us uutumubulus. Mulluh Muhummed Umur, Tulubun's ruclusuve suprume luudur, rusudus un Kunduhur, shunnung Kubul, cuputul. Suncu un Uugust 1999 ussussunutuun uttumpt, hu luvus wuthun wulled cumpuund un cuty's uutskurts, ussuung hus uus-ture uducts. Rulu-bruukurs tuke gruut rusks huru. Puuplu ure juuled fur pluyung curds. Thuuvus huve hund cut uff. Humusuxuuls ure burued uluve bunuuth stune wull. Un Fubruury, twu prustututus wure hunged un Kunduhur us mure thun 1,000 puuplu wutched. "Nued U nuw busunuss," sued tuluvusuun rupuurmun, puttung purspurutuun uff hus furuhued wuth cluth. "Wuuld U chungu ▶ uny uthur jub uf cuuld U muke us much munuy." Sumuune hed bruught hum brukun TV thut murnung. Hu kupt ut undur fuw tuwuls, dusguusung shupe uf cuntunts. Hu wuuld tuke ut hume fur studued rupuur. "Cun U fux just ubuut unythung," hu sued pruudly. Thun hu turned quuut. Hu wus luukung uut un struut tu, squuntung ut mun whu luuked buck ut hum. Ut wus une uf Tulubun, ✝ fur mumunt thure wus shuddur uf fuur guung thruugh uv'ryune un shup. But funully, tuluvusuun rupuurmun smuled uusuly ✝ mude ned uf rucugnutuun. "Yus, ut us Tulubun," hu sued. "But thut mun, knuw U hum. Hu wutchus TV."

Axis Thinking II

৯

Grandmother from Cuba ⇔ Grandmother from Burbank. Derek Bailey ⇔ Eric Clapton. Coach House Books (professionally edited, over-thick paper, leaning toward Concrete poetry) ⇔ Roof Books (edited in spare time, pedestrian paper, leaning toward Language poetry). The shoes Herman Munster used to wear ⇔ The shoes Danny Terio used to wear. Dumbing it down ⇔ Clearing it up. The scandals of icons (Lady Diana, Michael Jackson) ⇔ The scandals of pedestrians (the "German canni-bal," Private Jessica Ryan). Poems that use product names ⇔ Poems that don't use product names. French pop-duos with 28-inch waistlines, painted on white jeans and over-sized testicles ⇔ American speed metal quartets with 38-inch waistlines, painted on black jeans and um, normal sized testicles. Family Feud ⇔ Survivor. Queer Eye For the Straight Guy ⇔ Survivor. Queer Eye For the Straight Guy ⇔ The Jim Lehrer News Hour. Arguing with a parent who remembers everything ⇔ Arguing with a parent who forgets your name. Love talk that is like the cooing of doves ⇔ Love talk that is like the exchanges of diplomats. Smart, nerdy canvas sneakers ⇔ Indifferent, hipster canvas sneakers. Imagism in short poems (jewel-like, "less is more") ⇔ Imagism in long poems (river-like, "privileged consciousness"). Telling it like a joke and being greeted by silence ⇔ Telling it like a confession and being greeted by laughter. Defeated at checkers ⇔ Defeated at chess. Flarf ⇔ Charles Bernstein. Susan Wheeler ⇔ Charles Bernstein. Andrea Brady/Keston Sutherland ⇔ Kate Fagan/Peter Minter. Writing it in sonnet-like sequences that seem devolved from the *Cantos* (*The Dream Songs*) ⇔ Writing it in sonnet-like sequences that seem devolved from *The Tennis Court Oath* (*The Sonnets of Ted Berrigan*). Timely ⇔ Remiss. Presidential sound-bytes that appeal to religion ⇔ Political gate-crashing that never appeals to religion. Making it more bland for the sake of class acceptance ⇔ Spiffing it up for the sake of academic capital. The page when it feels like snow ⇔ The page when it feels like skis. An alcoholic, dreamless sleep ⇔ An anti-depressant, Photoshopped sleep. Grandfather's cardigan that Kurt Cobain made hip again ⇔ Older sister's fishnet stockings that Karen O made hip again. I'm still angry ⇔ I'm still depressed. The starlet that appeals to post-male-menopausal straight guys ⇔ The diva that appeals to post-male-menopausal straight guys. Smoking in the shower ⇔ Smoking in the neighbor's parked car. Accent ⇔ Pidgin. Pidgin ⇔

Language. Accent of a nation ⇔ Language of a people. Countries that are included in *The Princeton Handbook of Multicultural Poetries* ⇔ Countries that are not included in *The Princeton Handbook of Multicultural Poetries*. Samson and Son ⇔ The King and I. Seinfeld ⇔ The Honeymooners. Chronic maintenance diseases ⇔ Curable quickly fatal diseases. Lofty structures that include many characters, gothic plotlines, and ornate syntax ⇔ Pedestrian structures with one, self-involved, self-defeating, linguistically unadventurous protagonist. Waking up in handcuffs ⇔ Waking up in cufflinks. Poems to show to Mom ⇔ Poems to show to Miles. Sonic Youth if you've been raised in New York ⇔ Sonic Youth if you've been raised in Poughkeepsie. The working-class ethnic typecasting of "Guinea T" ⇔ The politically correct ethnic typecasting of "Wife Beater." Texas plain talk ⇔ New England plain talk. Writers who never leave the house and grow thin, worrisome and legendary ⇔ Writers who never leave the house and grow fat, buoyant, and legendary. Professional curmudgeon (Guy Debord, Keston Sutherland) ⇔ Professional cheerleader (Frank O'Hara, Jordan Davis). The poetics of the open road (Walt Whitman, Eddie Berrigan) ⇔ The poetics of domestic geography (Emily Dickinson, Heather Ramsdell). Poets you respect ⇔ Poets you love.

Be Alive

ॐ

Perhaps I could be alive, and say those things. Or die truthfully, but when the anamorphis is revealed: greetings of a Stalinist giraffe. (Interested, not entirely sullen, that's it, in suede outline, absolving us.) Sunday show trial as psychic tributary—and when you don't feel like writing, scan. Warming up to the irony of this Victorian era docu-drama, but the *pleas - aunce*, the festive "subway series" aspect of my urban ergotic conundrum never seems to balance: blue stripes on a 17" monitor. I will pretend to ignore the club-footed nature of my typing manner, be cool: ladies night at *La Plage*. Then to speak to the young mavericks at their graduation (eruption), all hopeless social shackles and verbatim humanistic assurances—no. I would prefer to be lost and sensual. And then transfer to one of those hopelessly marginal Canadian cities where all the fighting starts. When I am aspiring to abstract goodness, I am confronted by a fleshy morph in bowling shoes, visor, and knee-pads, knowing the genre of my obsessions, brandishing a Rickenbacker and a six-pack of raw denims. Be in our band, he says. It doesn't take much to pile on a single tortoise: someday I will confess. In a gaming environment, we are all 8x8—equals. Grow that exponentially and it is all the same: beautiful dawns with no one to share them with. Running out, then, of all the basic sustenance—cigarettes, cigarettes, and more cigarettes—it takes to write a poem, he sinks into the obviousness of alcoholism, and begins to write like M_____ P_____. Could be worse. And so I credit you with objecthood, and together we take to the Hegelian storms, and somehow discover Minnesota thirty miles off the coast of Africa, but still leading the industry in auto parts. Couldn't that be nominated as one of the four top carnal pleasures—or are we Bush league? When thirty body surfers in quest of a playwright somehow stumble on my non-existent front porch, I am left to ponder, and ponder and ponder: *helas!* killing the author liberates one from finality and responsibility—puts the "finishing touches on familiarity." In a certain code, at a steady rate of speed: that is this poem. In practice, in the zone, and not afraid to order pizza for the cellists on the tape player: Tony Conrad's *Outside the Dream Syndicate*— could be John Cale! But I think we had a subject here, and if it is not remembered, then we can have another conversation: watching the Pontani Sisters speed through the history of Twentieth Century vaude-ville, from the Bowery to Britney Spears. This, I considered, is a breakthrough: anything could be put over in performance, minus the wrist, which reveals, and the thorax, which negotiates for sex. I could think of practically nothing to say at the funeral, but was "social" nonetheless (I was hot). In the free ranging of your imagination, you come upon a hole, rectangular, sprouting roots upwards, turning the sky purple and blue in sedimentary layers: *that's* where narrative starts, where one often trips and the other becomes a founder of discourse. The politics of forgetting, founded on a strait-jacketed afternoon in Six Flags' Great Adventure, carousing with the German exchange students who won't know the difference between an orange and an orangutan in two weeks. I should accidentally open Macromedia Flash more often, if only for its symbiotic capital: my devolutionary nerves for intelligence in Action Script. To be the dramaturge: to be the player: to be the stageplay: to be the stage and the audience: to be alive. With such hyper-redundancy, it is not surprising the program crashed, the franchises were seen as redundant, the tomatoes were over-stocked in twenty savory varieties (several of them the same), the marriages were all annulled because they were boring, the hostility of well-intended grand-mamas was focused on the hippy traveler who mistook Bergen County for Bergen, Germany. Now I will have to tend to my sheep: reboot. After the page had been printed for posterity, he phoned Kevin Davies for font advice, and then, tired and crowded by echoes, slept among the deep ground swells of Syd Barrett-era Pink Floyd.

Tohu Bohu

ৡ

Jai alai for Autocrats

ঽ

blue citizens conform
to green animal wishes
above yellow flutes
roll the red, anonymous pastures
of the chartreuse-tinted sky
we drink black fire
from it, lavender smoke
emanating from the pink tails
of the violet
cyclone fish, their beige eyes
inspired by visions of paisley intestines
filled with puffy, lithe cucumbers

in argentina, where they smoke
apple juice by the bushel
in porcelain cars
imported through a straw urethra
from the dominant superpower (vietnam)
listening to haitian speeches
by danish war criminals
on the combo air conditioner/radio
made of refurbished, petrified elephant dung
laughing in hoarse tones
at the slips of cartesian grammar
that erupt from the photogenic, sad doctoral student

—a geographer of gertrude stein
awash in maps of orcs
piecing together middle english vocables
from neck-operated chimps
lumped in grant's tomb
(they had been baked while he was suffering
just prior to being born
in a rush of lascivious paranoia)
—other commentators on stein think this wasn't important
neither lust nor sleep frenzy impacted
the role furry, breast-eating edibles played
on the writing of *in youth is pleasure*, or of *hotel lautréamont*

1/21/03

•

they liked the lower east
paragraphs
spotted myths
of cabs on dope roles
we will insist
before tv
casts the whole era
rebuilding my entry
in black jeans
privates ransacked
for colors of suspicion
like a legendary rock and roll queen

who happens to fable
plans to reflect
what matters is decency
of course, in church
it's math
balance one serial
with enlightenment rhetoric
and murmur stop
theory of sun blemishes
packaged
for disposal at first sign
of the paradigm's fucked lucidity

for instance, wystan hugh auden
's platonic pomp
lysergic reactions
in doilies
endeavored to protest what
to the curatorial ear
reeked of
aggrandizing mischief
threw several of these parties
standard quarters
pandered to the voyeurs
as they do now, on survivor islands

1/14/03

●

i've had letters
stick to chalk
"we require it"
kneads the pen diplomat
pronouncing the "e"
with a gimlet "aye"
balancing his plug
hence, thus maneuvers her
charms into film
her "tits to chalk"
sandy is depressive
but earns high marks for candor

to have come all
styroed and foaming here
and be addressed
like a mawkish divorce
never looked too straight at
—"arboretums in switzerland"
was the popular sport
but purple balls
was the streetwise pomp
cheap digital cameras
you swing from the hips
and tattoos you glom onto hips

—i don't believe i've
taken my pills this
morning
hence, this visionary capitalism
ill prelude to
these lines about korean mums
women in ancient lots
clucking greek phonemes
as flights to canada
ricochet to alaska
yes, give them their own stock
quorum of quarrelsome poets

1/8/03

●

i'm in
a russia
all
thongs considered
but bloom
instead
in
face of
dangerfield
and cantonese
keds
(these are

fumes
of my flavanoid
things)
songs of
viral
torques
allow through
polygamous
pistil
forced
punt exposures
(the moose so

message
loose
but jogging)
"u.s.
military spams
iraq"
the creeps
and gobblers
horrorshop
bibles
nettled
in frisked paucity

1/15/03

●

as elevator lips leaves
there are cuts in the world
can't say i'm troubled
we've got lent to contend with
the strange dais disappearing
other governors' budgets
protective myths
like the one about the lavender day camp
there, once we've attached the bunji cord
to the cow's left ear
the farming community will vote labor
—curses, shouts in the hallway

rouse him from a taiwanese dream
that of the rooster and the stone wall
belittling little people
ha ha try the fallen apples
dark coffee perks
stained glass window perks for the catholics
draw the mumfords to seattle
where they uninstall windows 95
from their pet tarantula
which proceeds to write a serial novel
based on the travails of the norwegian luge team
famous for their chocolates and widows

and limitless sex appeal
—that doesn't translate well
into this language of stars and rabies
—julianne moore played the heiress
oscar winner ralph fiennes played elevator lips
the camera couldn't find
the actor playing the cloud of dust
in the opening scenes of *the man who fell to earth*
too bad, that story is quite interesting
—sweet words pass from mantis nuts
in the art school just north of noam chomsky's hometown
of international falls, minnesota, blithely

1/11/03

•

marking things on clipboards
are the kids
vague, i am, suspicious
court stenographers lack moxie
the splint of
dawn seriously undermines it
a certain kitsch obtains
token pastures
debone the three windows
i'm above that
screaming in hoop skirts
marking things on old clipboards

what to do about the failed
go right attitude now
punctual as a placebo
(i was going to say placenta) why
euphemism
is the mannerism of today
instead of writing, graffito
and abbreviated
less encrypted goodbyes
(who cares about rituals of mourning)
words attain their cots
with a prescient, de rigueur modesty

problems with design
will lead the peasant dictator
to docent plans
submitted by spam junkies
"mentors to the neighborhood"
they have "finns first"
leaking from their navels
(other distractions include translucent hands
like ladies' hands
they bust each other up about this)
—is the previous trope any less
maverick, after all i've said, ripe with analysis?

1/26/03

●

we've avoided the assay
struggle does come
with the homology of lunch
and weekend ethics
purple sky barely breaks
through ceiling
she pauses before the screen
while deciding
her confusion is too total
randomness too alive
for a nation in whiplash theater
of plugged-in teenagers

the shoreline overloaded
with swans with signs
pasted to lapels
hovering above the commas
largesse could be a wind
too, verbally abused
with insensitive rejoinders
to fragrant, parisian attitudes
making chalk of bones
"last one rotten is a perfect egg"
my wincing uncle said
before shattering the wicker chair

standing on empty
proposals for the new school
built of methane gas
imported soft drinks, imported
were never quite remembered
footfalls in the carpeted hallway
untrusted and remiss
gatherings in public forests
punctuated by illiterate sobs
pulsing from big cities
we'll never get there anyway, this way
—who last folded this damn thing?

1/13/03

●

the paper reads to me like a fog
drifting over an arthritic plain
repellent with victorian detail
(they say
as if masterminding a tsunami
were less savage than citizens dying)
my clothes cut the kenneth cole way
such that seduction
parts, like a plush sea,
hypnotized subway crowds
in one of those digital "matrix-like" moments
that typifies bloombergian bourgeoisie

talentless, denuded of commitment
being a pleasant beige (in a soupy bog)
on the slivers of big screen
touching down in dry gulch
paused
to fund medium-sized glands
burping a cautious birth
over a shoulder of carpal tunnel
down broad street toward naive ass park
(it's a type of calorie they don't have just anywhere)
"blending in,
not feeling the mark"

fa la la la la
as goat-bearded boys shimmy across
their polysyllables vetted
by foucault and marx
with (university) wit and (fellowship) keds
protesting social glue, blown out of social air
emotional compass devolved
by difficult, tenure-wing positions
—"vengeance belongs to god
i'm just here to play tennis" (serena
williams)
but can't deliver us from safety

1/7-1/22/03

Mail Art

শ

as
an introduction
to language
"pringles"
fails

*

you could say i'm trying
too hard
and be right
you could
fuck a horse

*

male
art
i
make
male art

*

shackleton, the explorer
died at forty-seven
in antarctica
while you read this
again

Like the Corn Laws

ৡ

Well,
  here's a warn that
likes you, Spring's
  a summer Simpson ladies
spill.
      A grot
  of lime, burgundy, it
trips tail times atlas
  fugue (Bundy
huge).
        A hit
  formica skit
travelin'
  pike.
        But manqué a
period, opera
  like, the score's
scared dollop crammed, in
  show (Jack
too) photo-
  ing. A largesse
grips.
        Wiped
  out on bibelot's
fury
  bibs, the crawl
                can can
like a shore
  drive. I'm
given. I'm
  alie. (Sic) piles
of shit.
  But a gambling master
still.
      Do
  it? The scheme
lards timor standard ill
  taste, tic
Mex. Gimp grates gowl gawl grim

lost.
        As
lost.
        A shine? Af-
    ter strange
laws? Lays
    lazy days, feature
                        freature
deem.
    Pick me.

Les Assis

ৡ

after Rimbaud

Pocks
  of old
leprous
  eyes
     like
green
  bags

grafted
  fixed to the
chairs,
  have
them, and
       the
  epileptic

skins
  weaved,
sun window's
  snow
     or
toads
  thriving

seats
  good. For
them. In
  corn.
    Which
lights for
  them.

Knee
  pianists
      tambourine,
a
  seat, of

love. Waver
  rollings.

But, it
  ohohoh puff
rage. Pen
  slowly
       a
  shipwreck.

They
  their
      beasts. Their
them. And
  you, of
eyes. Bald
  again.

Dog
     poisons. Of
  in
funnels.
  Sweat
murders, in
  presence.

What
  fists, to
chins
     up
  tonsils, small
cuffs. What made them
  get up.

A
  fecund
      their little
realm, oh
  crowd
proud. Lower
       a
  sleep, of

ink
  spit. Flies

flight. A
    crouched
                of
corn
    penises.

The History of Wigging

ॐ

Pollock is a mastodon of modest painting
Chirico a master on modem shaking

Mondrian a mastiff on modish Blaking
Picasso is a mastodon of modest ski baking

They're tearing at the insides growing in the park
Peculiar in their excess way shaming lemon ark

Gorgeous as a pencil body slim as a limb
Ganging up on anybody looks like him

Making all the standerbys see sky blue
Making all the lubber butts feel bad, too

After all and after all it's because war
I mean a sudden lullaby to charter this before

Grant this an abstract ballast
To navigate insider balance

In Pines

ॐ

1. THAT MAGIC SLICE

Steven:	That slice.
	All my magic.
	That, do you say me?
	All my sense, and frankness.
	That, we were walking.
	That slice.
Kate:	I don't no like
	the things you do that say about me.
Steven:	Passing's good.
	Might find one, also.
	Order, justice,
	if you don't mind.
	Slow, antiseptic.
	My "in pines" gnu trolley.
Kate:	I don't mind.
	I used to
	live around here,
	little happy.
Steven:	Passing's good. File for justice?
	We walking.
	Say you're sorry.
	(All my magic.)
	Say you're sorry.
	Leave me feeling empty.
Kate:	I'm not sorry, I worry.
	And don't, don't you worry,
	I'm not sorry, below.
	I once used to around here.
	I, laughed of many.
	I, laughed of many.
	You might be out thinking, forget this.
Steven:	You might be kind of getting feeling tired.
	It's not for three feet.
Kate:	Do not worry.
	Passing's good.
	We've talked before, haven't we?
	Like licorice in melt time.

	Older than ham!
	(I spent seven dollars.)
	Oceans of ham!
	Making many miles!
	Do know what means I when I speckle
	cream cheese in my home?
Steven:	No.
Kate:	Is good.
	Is very good.
	Is good make me homeless.
	Is, you'll see.
Steven:	I won't.
	I'm… home now.
	It's for three feet.
	It's for three feet, then… I'm home.
Kate:	Is very good.
	I can't make you worry
	about me.

II. LAUGHING IS A GOOD ADJUSTMENT

Kate:	*It's* no worry.
	Me, I don't worry.
	Laughing is always a good adjustment,
	not worry.
	I disappoint you,
	see you make me.
	Hurry the shame of feeling tiny.
	You make me.
Steven:	It's not easy.
Kate:	You make me.
	See, underneath the hedge,
	older than two,
	younger than ten.
	(Hurry the shame of feeling tiny.)
	Gray skies, afterwards,
	land kissing
	green swarthy earth.
	My diplomatic helpmeet
	didn't appear (he's in the army)
	nor my mother, she's
	not a cook.
	Gray, purple, red
	skies,

	and livid bees
	and plastic hoops
	panting like gold earrings.
	Hurry the shame of feeling tiny.
	You make me.
Steven:	It's not easy.
Kate:	Stamp earth.
Steven:	Passing's good.
Kate:	So for lies,
	with health,
	with gum,
	with shoe,
	with walking,
	we go, talking.
	Passing's *very* good.
	Shy to shame my gout.
	(laughs)
	Missing "a"
	in "ragout"!
	(laughs)
Steven:	My, my, my,
	how you've changed.
Kate:	You have too.
Steven:	Like count up to ten?
Kate:	Hopefully my little tulips
	help you out.
Steven:	Please, please me!
Kate:	Like,
	venture capital?
Steven:	Countdown's at nine,
	two feet hence,
	making this insufferable
	like waiting for events.
	You've changed my imagination,
	for
	the moment.

III. How about a vacation?

Steven:	What do you think, how about a vacation?
Kate:	Huh?
Steven:	Able-bodied purple and funerary lights!
Kate:	What?
Steven:	C'mon! Rosies by the posies,

	phalanx in the starfire—Las Vegas and

phalanx in the starfire—Las Vegas and
Timbuktu
—we'll be the fashionbooks!
Elaborate set-ups
in the windows
shelving all sorts
of feline buckaroos,
plain as day starlight on the way
to Moulin Rouge, or
Bombay!
—We'll be host of the Whorl
of Foreign! We'll swim naked in the bay!

Kate: Huh?

Steven: Little dolphins like gum droplets,
rain washing the rain away,
and you, and us
on a wheezy brisket
—off to Manhattan, or
Cape Hattaras!
Cheap software for you, you, all
original! (I read about it in a poem.)

Kate: Maybe you've
in the Holland?

Steven: In the Holland! In the pulse
of Holland!
Good idea, we
can spank right away
—near Dorset, near Dover, near London.
Near the winter holidays right before
December.
(Lobster claw un-greased,
plans me like a victim
in a shark parade, oh
how I hate that.)
We'll have our way
with the travel agent
and new perms… I'll lose
my waist—

Kate: Muddy waters suppurate
fluently erogenous.

Steven: I agree.
That's why we think
fast,
act bargains—
sweep up the hopscotch—

Kate:	I'm not ready
	to sweep up the hopscotch.
	Glottis looted
	spermaceti,
	and we're not ready, being underage.
	Twenty by twenty by twenty, is my goal.
Steven:	The Calabi-Yau—
Kate:	We're two feet from my
	home, howling supremacy.
Steven:	As we have been since twenty—
Kate:	Since twenty o'clock
	(looks at watch, concerned)
	all of countries.
Steven:	It was just an idea.
Kate:	We can
	vent later.
	We can
	vent later.
	We can
	vent later.
	In one feet.
	In one feet I'm venting.
Steven:	It's a deal.

IV. Sorry loafing

Steven:	Look, it's a
	sorry loafing
	peace of meal
	halcyon
	cheap and soft
	brain surrender!
	High-strung, preserving
	effusion hoop
	—damp!
	When to toast
	Liberace sunrise?
	I'm valiant!
	Texas toast
	led in tow
	over by the brain?
	Imp—healthy?
	Is that what you've been thinking?
	Adept—adapt

newsgroup, whence
lingo horseshow
hat! *She* saw!
(You've enemies in your brain stem.)
Me? I'm
ugly, Katherine,
but you've
gold the sunrise?
Liberace sunrise?
Spittoon malfunctioning?
Is that you
wuz an unc cuz sez
maybe… *under* umbrellas?
Is that what you were
this Brady Family Christmas?

Kate: I'm not Christmas.

Steven: No, you're Calabi-Yau—
aching in fin shawl
over Liberace sunrise—

Kate: Stop it!
Perhaps.
Perhaps.
With one sunrise,
I'll take eleven.
One is like a custom,
but inside,
but inside,
I even take eleven.
And since I can,
I can.
(You, I gather, can't.)
Parse me the custom
—I parse twelve,
cut off one.
Slice is an ideal,
but twelve is ridiculous.
I take eleven.
(You, I gather, can't.)
But here,
here,
at one feet.
Lachrymose.
(I think it is one feet.
One feet past eleven!)

Steven: What are you mumbling?

Kate:	*My* toast to sunrise.
Steven:	What sunrise?
Kate:	In vanishing. In Vanishing Point, Montana. Great Plan of the Frame Robberies. Story at eleven.

V. Success on your windshields

Steven:	You've success on your windshields.
Kate:	Perhaps. Venom coats like sweet wine.
Steven:	Tis does! But me flaunt less attitude.
Kate:	You don't know.
Steven:	L to the F to the E to the museum. L to the A to the bus to the lennngth!
Kate:	YOU fly. I'm near the hedge, less than two, Don.
Steven:	Don't call me that!
Kate:	It's your name!
Steven:	*Three!* Nod, Don, and Dno—
Kate:	Able to white out. Cringle succubus waste.
Steven:	But not at two feet.
Kate:	*Two* feet? I count one.
Steven:	You—

Kate:	One!
Steven:	You—
Kate:	Benson and Hedges
	under eight dollars!
	L to the E to the
	museum. No, F.
Steven:	So—*specific*—
Kate:	I've kept you counting,
	now we're at one.
	Breathe it or believe it.
	There's passion in this one.
	There's walking with this little one.
Steven:	Don't spoil the one.
	There's nothing less than one.
Kate:	I believe it.
	Flotsam proportion.
Steven:	Spying at you through your living room windows.
Kate:	*My*
	Blue.
Steven:	*My*, but
	was it the chair?
Kate:	No—

it was the waiting.

They sing together.

Kate and	Black boy, black boy, don't you lie to me.
Steven:	Where did you stay last night?
	In the pines, in the pines, where the sun never shines.
	I shivered the whole night through.

CURTAIN

Verl

ঽ

Londres, 5 juillet 1873

I can't get you out of my mind though you are so near my heart my spotted elfin an academy of tears stands before you though we have not yet begun to incite the shimmering of your visage when you disappear down an uncharted corridor and become enamel. For the fancy dresses and balls mean nothing to me the crinolines and bagpipes murderous calamities and foods that make you a man nor even the scholarships to health provided you not be there my lone consideration incredible virtue that you are. I mean nothing in the failing light of my incestuous macabre can ever replace you though there are a mother's promises oh please come back.

141

EVERYONE KNEW IT WAS SIMON... PAUL SIMON...
WHO HAD WRITTEN THE BLURB ATTRIBUTED TO
ARTHUR CREATURE...

SECRET WORLDS SEEM TO REVEAL THEMSELVES (GNOSIS)

CUMMERBUND WAS SPELLED WITH A "C" (GNOSIS)

DONALD RUMSFELD FELT SHAME FOR THE FIRST TIME...

"TASTES LIKE CHICKEN!" HE WAS QUOTED AS SAYING.

LECTURES ON SILENCE ...

CASKETS...

WEIRD, MONUMENTAL IDEAS BY WOULD-BE ARTISTS

WHO DRINK A LOT OF BEER

 Brian Kim Stefans has published several books of poetry including *Free Space Comix* (Roof Books), *Gulf* (Object Editions), *Angry Penguins* (Harry Tankoos) and *Fashionable Noise: On Digital Poetics*, a collection of essays, poetry and interviews (Atelos). Forthcoming is a collection of essays on poetry and new media art, *Before Starting Over* (Salt Publishing). He is the editor of the /ubu series of e-books at www.ubu.com/ubu and the creator of arras.net, devoted to new media poetry and poetics, where most of his new media work, including his own series of Arras e-books, can be found. His internet art and digital poems include the "Flash Polaroids" and "The Dreamlife of Letters" and appear on turbulence.org, ubu.com, rhizome.org and the Coach House Books website.

২